1-Hour WordPress 2018

A visual step-by-step guide to building WordPress websites in one hour or less!

Dr. Andy Williams

http://ezseonews.com

Updated 19th December 2017

"I work in the education department at one of the top academic institutions in the U.S. and if I could hire Dr. Williams to write all of my online training, I wouldn't hesitate." Laura

Contents

What people are saying about previous versions of this book:

"Complete, quick, and to the point. Just what most people need. Good information. No filler. Great price. A well thought out book by Dr. Andy Williams" **Zoie Brytin**

"This guide or more accurately a manual is an excellent training guide by a teacher that I have been learning from for many years. It is well written and laid out and will help you learn WordPress without stress. Highly recommended." **Dale Reardon**

"By following the steps in the book, you'll easily have your WordPress site up & running in no time and, as Andy knows his stuff, you can be confident it will be set up well." **SBUK**

"Great content from a great author! Highly recommended!" **David H**

"I have read articles which say just set up a WordPress blog and I haven't the faintest idea but this book is very simply and carefully written so no steps are left out. Andy is an expert who seems to be able to explain things in a way which helps the non-expert. A rare talent. It gave me the confidence to have a go." **Chris Wade**

"I think everyone thinking of building a WordPress website should read this guide first. I've been using WordPress for several years and I am amazed at how much I didn't know about WordPress. The guide takes you through the whole process of getting web hosting, buying a domain name, designing your website to help with Seach Engine Optimisation and everything else you need to know about posts versus pages, widgets, plugins and lots more. Dr.Andy has a very pleasant writing style which concentrates on what to do and why to do it, without making lots of unnecessary remarks just to fill out a few more pages. And the bonus is that readers get access to his website which he built alongside writing the book and he plans to provide a lot more relevant information there in the future." **John D Bridson**

"The step by step approach is excellent." **Carole**

"Doing anything for the first time can be daunting. Putting up your first WordPress site is no different - especially for the software challenged. Luckily this book offers an easy-to-follow step-by-step process covering all that is needed to overcome any lack of previous experience. With this guide in hand, a new site can realistically be in place in a matter of hours." **John Gergye**

"With this product, it was as if he read my mind (or was watching over my shoulder). " Alan **Northcott**

"The first thing I want to say about "Rapid WordPress Websites" is that you should download it immediately because you need to look no further for information about building your first WordPress website." **Norman Morrison**

"Dr. Andy walks you through the WordPress setup process, step by step. He explains the why's of the steps you are taking, what to do, how to do it, and why you should do it. "Rapid WordPress Websites" is a great instructional refresher guide for even the Pro." **E. W. Aldridge, Sr**

"Anyone who gets this book and follows the steps will be able to have their own website up and running in no time. I hadn't installed a WP blog in years and had forgotten how to do it. Dr. Andy's book made the process simple and painless." **J. Tanner**

"I have been struggling with my WordPress Website - not anymore. This is a must-read for beginners and I bet even some long-time user will find information in Andy's book. I now realize how little I knew about WordPress, the great thing about this book is it walks you by the hand to get your site going and getting down to business. This is one of those books that you will refer to time and time again. So keep it handy!" **Suzanne Dean**

DISCLAIMER AND TERMS OF USE AGREEMENT

Introduction

Firstly, thank you for buying my book.

This book used to be called "Rapid WordPress Websites". The reason I changed the title of this latest update is simple. I wanted to highlight the fact that you can have your very own WordPress website in an hour or less, from now.

Yes, really.

The aim of this book is to teach anybody (even complete non-techie beginners) to create a website quickly by working through the book, chapter by chapter.

I have written other books on WordPress, but this one is special. The emphasis in this one is to teach you on a need-to-know basis and not try to cover everything that WordPress can do (my WordPress for Beginners book & course both do that).

If you want to learn more about WordPress, a good place to start is my ezSEONews.com website. You'll find a lot of articles, news, and discussion, on a wide range of topics related to WordPress.

http://ezseonews.com

Special Offer on Video Course

For those that like to learn WordPress in a more interactive way, I've created several WordPress courses which I run on the Udemy learning platform. These range from WordPress "essentials" that directly complement this book, to the more comprehensive and specialist courses on WordPress. You can see what courses are available here:

http://ezseonews.com/courses

Found Typos in this book?

Errors can get through proof-readers, so if you do find any typos or grammatical errors in this book, I'd be very grateful if you could let me know using this email address:

typos@ezseonews.com

WordPress.com v WordPress.org

The first thing that confuses many WordPress students is that there are two types of WordPress. These are found on two separate websites.

If you visit WordPress.com, you can sign up to create a WordPress site for free. WordPress.com hosts your site on their servers, meaning you do not need to buy a domain, or hosting. The downside is that there are limitations. WordPress.com controls what you can and cannot do on your site. For example, you won't be able to customize WordPress in the way you want, because you cannot just install any theme or plugin you want. You also won't be using your own domain name. Your website address will be something like:

myhealthsite.WordPress.com

This type of domain is called a sub-domain and it is hosted on the WordPress.com website. Therefore, you do not own the domain and WordPress.com could theoretically close your site down if they think you are abusing their terms of service.

There are paid options on WordPress.com which allow you to use your own domain, but the price for doing so is greater than if you just use WordPress.org in the first place and unless you are on the most expensive plan, there will still be restrictions.

I don't recommend WordPress.com for building sites, but if you decide you want to try, I have a course on using this free service. You can find discounted links to all my courses at the end of this book.

WordPress.org, on the other hand, is a site where you can download the WordPress software for yourself, to install on a server of your choice, and customize it however you wish. This allows you to create a website that you own, and you can do whatever you want on it. You also get to choose your own domain name, like:

myhealthsite.com

Doesn't that look better? Be aware that domain names are on a strictly first come, first served basis. You obviously cannot choose a domain name that someone else already owns.

In this book, we are using the WordPress from WordPress.org, buying a domain name, and building the site on our own web host.

NOTE: It is possible to install WordPress on your own computer if you just want to learn without the expense of buying a domain and subscribing to a web host. Obviously, that is beyond the scope of this book, so check out those courses (the one called "Installing WordPress Locally") at the end of this book if you are interested.

Let's get started...

Domains, Registrars & Hosting

Your domain name is important to you. It will be your website address where you can send your friends & family to view your site. It is the website address that Google and other search engines will send people to. Therefore, choosing a domain name is important, and you want to get it right the first time. You cannot get a refund on a purchased domain name if you find you made a spelling mistake or changed your mind about the name.

Two types of domain name

There are two main types of domain name. The first category, which I suggest you avoid, is often referred to as "Exact Match Domain", or EMD for short.

An EMD is a domain name that exactly matches a phrase you want to rank for in Google. For example, if you decide you wanted to be #1 on Google when anyone searched for "Healthy Coconut Oil", then an EMD would be something like:

- Healthycoconutoil.com
- Healthy-coconut-oil.com
- Healthcocounutoil.org

See how the exact phrase makes up the domain name?

This used to work well in Google, and in the past, we could easily rank sites for phrases by choosing an EMD for the phrase we were interested in. However, things have changed. EMDs can cause you problems, including getting your site penalized in Google, or even banned if you are not careful.

I, therefore, suggest you choose my second category of domain name – a brandable name.

A brandable domain name is one that is memorable and could be used as branding. Think of Google itself. This is a brand name we all recognize, but what would have happened if they had chosen "best search engine" as an EMD? Bestsearchengine.com doesn't have the same ring to it, does it?

I recommend you sit down and think about your domain name carefully. Avoid choosing a name simply because it contains a phrase you want to rank for. Instead, think of a memorable name that people will remember when they hear it.

Imagine being out and about and you see a friend. You want to send them over to look at your new website but you don't have a pencil to write the name down. The domain name you choose should be memorable enough that your friend can remember it once you tell them.

TLDs

TLD stands for Top Level Domain and simply refers to the extension given to your domain. Possible TLDs include .com, .org, .net, .co.uk, .de etc. There are new TLDs coming out on a regular basis and it can all be confusing for beginners.

Some TLDs are country-specific, e.g. .co.uk is used for websites targeting the UK.

My advice on choosing a TLD is simple.

If you only want to target one country with your site, choose the TLD for that country:

.es for Spain

.co.uk for the UK

.de for Germany

If your site has global appeal, choose a .com.

How much is it all going to cost?

Since we need to buy a domain and hosting, you may already be wondering how much this is going to cost. Let me break it down for you:

You need to buy a domain name which will cost around $9.99 per year. You buy domain names from "domain registrars" (see below).

You need to get web hosting, and that costs from around $3.99 per month. You buy web hosting from a "web host" (see below).

These are your only required costs, though obviously, you can decide to buy a premium WordPress theme and maybe some commercial plugins. However, these are not required, and you can build a great looking, feature-packed site, without any additional costs.

Your total essential costs for a self-hosted website will be around $58 per year. That's not bad considering you'll be able to get your message out to the entire connected world.

What is a Domain Registrar?

A domain registrar is a company that you buy your domain name from. Good registrars will make sure your domain auto-renews at the end of the year, can keep your site "anonymous", lock your domain so it cannot be transferred to another individual without your approval, and a lot of other administrative stuff.

What is a Web host?

A web host is a company that rents out computer space to anyone that wants to create their own website. They are responsible for making sure your site is up and running 24/7. All websites can go down at times (as I am sure you have seen), but good web hosts will have your website up and running 99.9% of the time.

All-in-one registrar and web host?

Most web hosts will also offer to be your domain registrar. In other words, they look after everything for you. The advantage of this is that everything is in one place, and you are only dealing with one company.

The disadvantage of this is that if you have problems with your host, they hold all the cards, and can make moving away from them difficult. I have heard horror stories about some hosts.

The thing about web hosts is that they might be great today, but suck tomorrow. I have seen several great hosts go downhill quickly. Being able to move your site quickly if you ever need to is important.

I want you to avoid potential problems down the line by doing things right from the start, so I am going to show you how to use a separate host and registrar.

Before you start thinking that a separate registrar and host is more complicated, it really isn't. It's also no more expensive. In fact, the registrar I will recommend to you is free to use.

I will show you how to painlessly and easily set up your domain so that that you are using a separate domain registrar and hosting company. You are then in control. If you ever need to move from one web host to another, the process is very simple, and your site can be moved within hours, with zero downtime.

My Recommended Web Host and Registrar

As you might guess from the information above, I do change my web hosts occasionally. What I recommend today may not be what I recommend in a year's time. Therefore, to make sure you are using the absolute best services that I know of (the ones I personally use), I recommend you visit my page here to check:

http://ezseonews.com/host

I will keep it updated if there are any changes.

At the time of writing this book, my chosen registrar is Namecheap and my chosen Web host is StableHost. I have been happily using both for several years now, without issue. I will show you how to set up a site using these two services (and even get you a 40% discount on your web hosting).

Visit http://ezseonews.com/host

Click on the link for my recommended Registrar. Sign up for a free account. Once you have that account set up, come back here and we will continue.

Buying the domain at the registrar

Over at the registrar (Namecheap), we want to buy a new domain.

From the Domains menu at the top, select **Domain Name Search**:

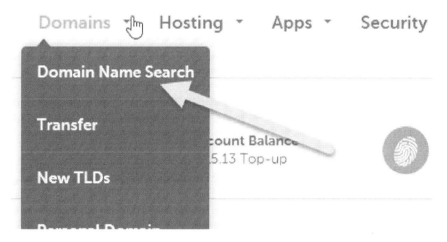

You can then type in your chosen domain name (with TLD) and click the search button to see if it is available.

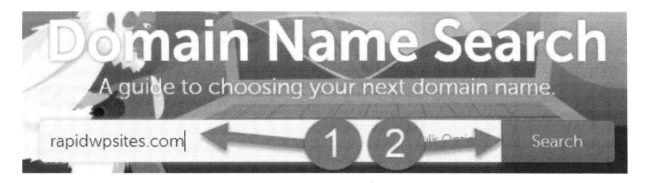

My chosen domain is available:

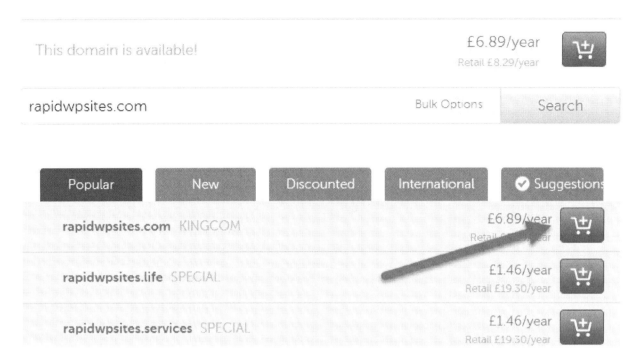

Click the shopping trolley button to buy the domain.

The domain will be added to your cart. View the cart and make sure your domain is correct (check the spelling), and then buy it.

At the checkout, make sure you select Auto-Renew for the domain.

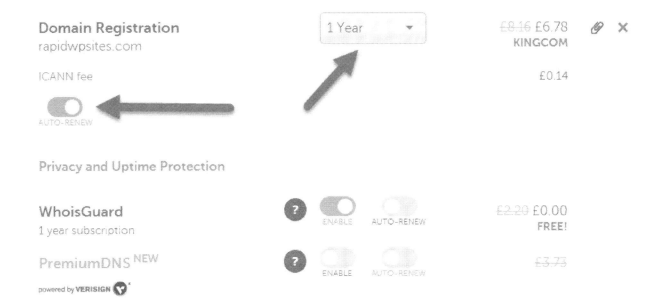

This will ensure that the registrar will automatically renew your domain name each year (until you cancel). Failure to renew a domain will result in your domain being released when the year is up, and someone else will be able to buy it.

When you buy your domain, you can buy it for longer than one year if you want to. If you have auto-renew enabled, I see no reason to buy for longer than one year.

Also, you may be offered free WhoisGuard. This service is only free for the first year.

WhoisGuard protects your name, address, phone number and other contact details from the Whois.net database. Anyone can search this database online (at http://whois.net) to find contact details for the owner of a website. If you want the privacy, this is a good option to include.

When you are happy with your selection, click the confirm order button to buy your domain.

If you got the WhoisGuard as well, there will be a link asking you to activate it on the domain. Just follow the instructions there.

OK; that's the registrar done.

Let's head over to the web hosting company.

Visit this page again, and click through to the recommended web host:

http://ezseonews.com/host

If my recommendation is still StableHost, check for a discount code I've included on that page which will give you a 40% discount on hosting (I cannot guarantee how long this will be available).

Buying Web hosting

On the web hosting page, which you can access from the menu across the top, you can sign up for hosting:

I recommend you use the Starter plan, to begin with. If your site becomes very popular, or you decide to build other sites, you can always upgrade to a more comprehensive plan when you need to.

When you click the **Sign Up Now** button, you will be taken to the product selection screen:

Product Selection: Web Hosting Plans - Unlimited Starter

Please provide us with the domain you want to use with your hosting service by selecting an option from the selections below.

Select the option to use your existing domain and update name servers as this one lets you use a different registrar. Enter the domain name and the extension in the two boxes provided. Note that it looks like the TLD (.com) is already entered, but it isn't. You need to enter that as well.

Click the **Continue** button to choose billing cycle.

Web hosts often give incentives for paying for hosting up front. With Stablehost, as I write this, if you only want to sign up for 6 months, it will cost you $4.95 per month. However, if you pay for 36 months up front, it'll only cost you $3.50 per month.

I recommend paying for as long a period as you feel comfortable with, as any discount you get from the coupon on my site will apply to the amount you are paying now. I'll select 36 months to show you.

The only other option you need to choose here is the hosting location. You can choose from Phoenix, Amsterdam, Chicago and Singapore. Your website will be served from the server in the location you choose, so select the place closest to where you think your target audience is located. If you are unsure, just select Phoenix.

You don't need to worry about any "available add-ons" with your hosting. You don't need these.

Click on the **Continue** button and you'll be taken to the **Review & Checkout** screen:

Review & Checkout

ion	Price
es.com)	
	$126.00 USD
Subtotal:	$126.00 USD
Total Due Today:	$126.00 USD
Total Recurring:	$126.00 USD Triennially

As you can see, the full cost for 36 months hosting is 126.00. However, remember that coupon code. Enter that in the promotional code box on the page.

..and you'll see 40% discount applied to that total:

Review & Checkout

ion	Price
s.com)	
	$126.00 USD
Subtotal:	$126.00 USD
40% One Time Discount:	$50.40 USD
Total Due Today:	$75.60 USD
Total Recurring:	$126.00 USD Triennially

The above screenshot shows that the promotional code would save me over $50 on this hosting package.

Instead of costing $126.00, it's just $75.60!

Go through to the checkout and pay for your hosting.

It may take a few hours for your hosting to be set up. Once it is, the host will email you will login details for your cPanel (which you'll need for setting up WordPress). You will also have login details for your "Client Login", and it's in there you can get support if you need it.

The other thing you'll get in your welcome email is the Server information. This is what you are looking for:

Server Information

Server Name: en01.stablehost.com

If you are using an existing domain with your new hosting ac
below.

Nameserver 1 ns1.stablehost.com (199.192.218.10)
Nameserver 2 ns2.stablehost.com (199.192.219.10)

Uploading Your Website

There are two Nameservers. If you are using the same host as me, they'll be the same as in the screenshot above.

We will need these in the next step.

Connecting the Registrar and host

Login to your registrar (Namecheap).

From the menu on the top left, select **Domain List**.

You will see your domain listed. Click on the **Manage** button to the right of the domain name.

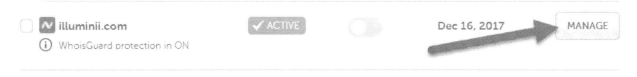

You will be on the **Domain** tab, so scroll down until you see the Nameservers section:

Make sure **Custom DNS** is selected at the top of this section and then enter the two nameservers (that we located in the previous section) in boxes 1 & 2.

Finally, click the **Save** button that looks like a little check mark (tick).

That's it. The registrar and the web host will now work together. Not that difficult, was it?

Now we can go and install WordPress on the domain.

Installing WordPress

For this, you need to login to the cPanel of your hosting. The URL, username, and password were all in that welcome email the host sent to you.

Once you are logged in, scroll down to the **Softaculous Apps Installer** section, and click on **Softaculous Apps Installer**.

On the next screen, you'll see a box containing the WordPress logo. Move your mouse over it, and an **Install** button will appear:

Click the **Install** button.

At the top of the next screen, you'll see the **Software Setup**:

Software Setup

Choose Protocol

If your site has SSL, then please choose the HTTPS protocol.

Choose Domain

Please choose the domain to install the software.

In Directory

The directory is relative to your domain and should not exist. e.g. To install at http://mydomain/dir/ just type dir. To install only in http://mydomain/ leave this empty.

http://

harlun.co.uk

In the **Choose Protocol** box, select http://

In the **Choose Domain** box, select your domain.

Clear the **In Directory** box by deleting the pre-filled value.

The next section of this screen is the **Site Settings**.

Site Settings

Site Name

Site Description

Enable Multisite (WPMU) 🛈

Harlun Limited

My Company Website

Enter a name and short description (tagline) for your site. Don't worry, you can change these later.

Make sure **Enable Multisite** is unchecked.

In the **Admin Account** section, enter a username, password, and the email address you want to use for this website.

Admin Account

Admin Username

admin

Admin Password

pass

Hide 🔍

Bad (18/100)

Admin Email

admin@harlun.co.uk

Do not use "admin" as the username. Use something a little harder to guess, and the same goes for the password.

The next section allows you to choose your language and then there is a **Select Plugin** section.

The plugin that is available is called Limit Login Attempts, and it can help prevent hackers gaining access to your site, so check that box.

Select Plugin(s)

Limit Login Attempts (Loginizer) ⓘ   ☑

The final section on this page is the **Advanced Options**. Open them by clicking the "+".

➕ Advanced Options

I recommend you enable the following:

- Auto Upgrade
- Auto Upgrade WordPress Plugins
- Auto Upgrade WordPress Themes

Finally, before clicking the **Install** button, enter an email address to receive the installation details. Once WordPress is installed, the username and password will be sent to this address.

With all that complete, click the **Install** button.

Once the installation has finished, you'll be shown something like this:

Congratulations, the software was installed successfully

WordPress has been successfully installed at :
http://harlun.co.uk
Administrative URL : http://harlun.co.uk/wp-admin/

We hope the installation process was easy.

The first link will load your website which is now actually online. Congratulations! It may not be much yet, but you have created your very first WordPress website!

Here is mine:

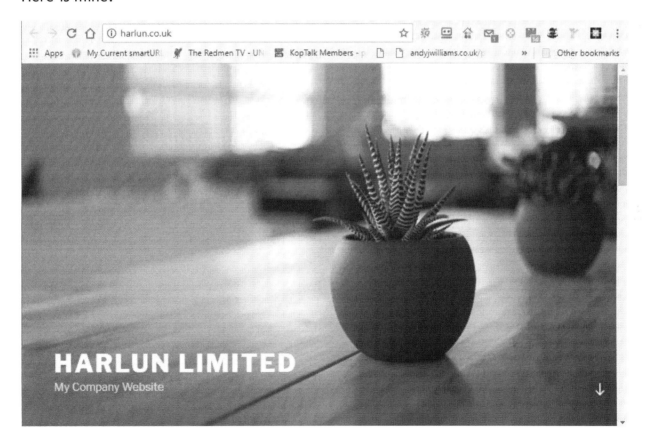

The default WordPress site you see will use the current WordPress default "theme". Think of a theme as a skin to your site, that can be changed. Every theme is different, and by changing the theme, you can change the entire look and feel of your website.

At the time of writing this, the default theme was Twenty Seventeen, so that is the theme you see in the screenshot above. Yours may show a different theme, but that is fine. You'll want to play with themes later and choose one that you like.

The second URL listed is the Administrative URL.

Congratulations, the software was installed successfully

WordPress has been successfully installed at :
http://harlun.co.uk
Administrative URL : http://harlun.co.uk/wp-admin/

You can click that link to login to the WordPress Dashboard for your site.

Bookmark the URL for your Dashboard. You will need it whenever you want to go in and work on your website.

The username and password are those that you used when filling in the Admin Details a few minutes ago.

OK, let's log in to the Dashboard.

Login and Logout of your WordPress Dashboard

The WordPress Dashboard is where you go to add content and customize the look of your site. Think of it as the control center for your website.

You should have bookmarked the URL already, but if you ever forget or lose your admin link, just add **/wp-admin/** to the end of your domain URL.

This is what the login page looks like:

Enter your Admin username and Admin password. I recommend you check the **Remember Me** box so that it remembers your login details next time.

Now click the **Log In** button.

You will be taken inside the dashboard. Here is mine:

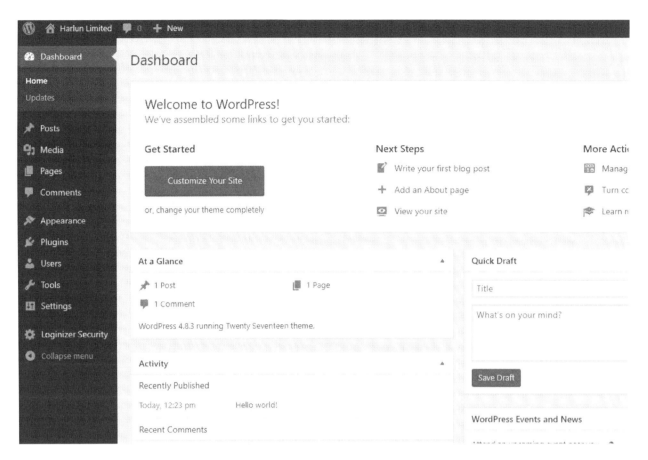

OK, this is where the fun starts.

Looking at the demo page, post, and comment

.. and deleting them

When you install WordPress you will get some demo content installed by default. This includes:

- A post
- A page
- A comment

Don't worry about posts and pages, we will discuss them later. For now, let's take a quick look.

Visit your site in a web browser. You can do this in a number of different ways.

Obviously, you can type the domain URL into the web browser.

If you are already in your dashboard, move your mouse over your domain name (top left). Now right-click the **Visit** Site link and select **Open link in a new tab.**

Your website will open in a new tab.

This is your homepage and you should see a post titled "Hello World".

Hello world! ⬅

Welcome to WordPress. This is your first post. Edit or delete it, then start writing!

A note on the homepage

The homepage is a special page. By default, WordPress will show your most recent 10 posts on the homepage (there is only one on your homepage right now because there is only one post on your site – the "Hello World" post).

The homepage can display the full post(s), or what is called excerpts. What it shows depends on the WordPress theme you are using and how you set it up. While the latest posts appear on the Homepage, you should also know that they also each appear on their own "post page". If you click the "Hello World!" title shown in the screenshot above, you will be taken to the post's page.

This page contains the single post in its entirety, any comments on the post, and a "Leave a Reply" comment box for visitors to leave a comment.

Here is the "Hello World!" post page on my site:

Hello world!

Welcome to WordPress. This is your first post. Edit or delete it, then start writing!

Edit

One Reply to "Hello world!"

A WordPress Commenter

NOVEMBER 2, 2017 AT 12:23 PM   EDIT

Hi, this is a comment.
To get started with moderating, editing, and deleting comments, please visit the Comments screen in the dashboard.
Commenter avatars come from Gravatar.

↰ **Reply**

Leave a Reply

Logged in a: og out?

Comment

NOTE: If you don't like the idea of the homepage showing the last 10 posts, and you'd rather have a carefully crafted homepage "article", you can do that. I'll show you how to set up a static homepage soon.

If you go back to the homepage, you'll see a sidebar. In the Twenty Seventeen theme, the sidebar is on the right.

Search …   🔍

RECENT POSTS

Hello world!

RECENT COMMENTS

A WordPress Commenter on Hello world!

ARCHIVES

November 2017

CATEGORIES

Uncategorized

META

Site Admin

Log out

Some themes will have the sidebar on the left, and others won't have a sidebar.

You can see that "Hello World!" is listed in the sidebar in a section called **Recent Posts**.

There is also a section called **Recent Comments**, with one entry:

RECENT COMMENTS

A WordPress Commenter on Hello world!

When WordPress was installed, it added this "Hello World!" post and the comment (on that post) as a kind of demo for you. If you go to the Hello World post page, you can see the comment at the end:

One Reply to "Hello world!"

A WordPress Commenter

NOVEMBER 2, 2017 AT 12:23 PM   EDIT

Hi, this is a comment.
To get started with moderating, editing, and deleting comments, please visit the Comments screen in the dashboard.
Commenter avatars come from Gravatar.

↩ **Reply**

Leave a Reply

Logged in as   Log out?

Comment

You'll also see other sections in the sidebar, including Archives, Categories, and Meta. These sidebar sections are inserted into the sidebar using something called "Widgets". We'll look at these later, but just so you know, you can add or delete widgets in the sidebar, so it is highly customizable.

When you installed WordPress, a "Page" was also installed. We can find that in the dashboard, as well as the post and comment.

Login to the Dashboard.

A quick way to get into the Dashboard is to use the admin bar across the top. This will appear when you are viewing your site but logged into the dashboard already. Here it is:

Move your mouse over the domain name and click on **Dashboard** to get in.

On logging in, you'll have a menu down the left:

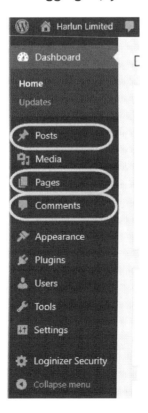

You can see the menu items for "Posts", "Pages" and "Comments".

Click on the Posts menu item and you'll be taken to a screen listing all posts on the site.

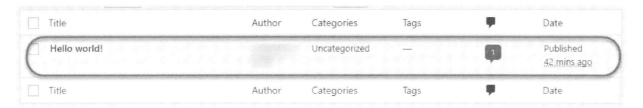

Now, there's only one - the "Hello World" post. No surprise there as we haven't added any yet. If you want to go in and edit the Hello World post, click on the title and you'll be taken to the post edit screen.

OK, click on the "Comments" menu in the left sidebar.

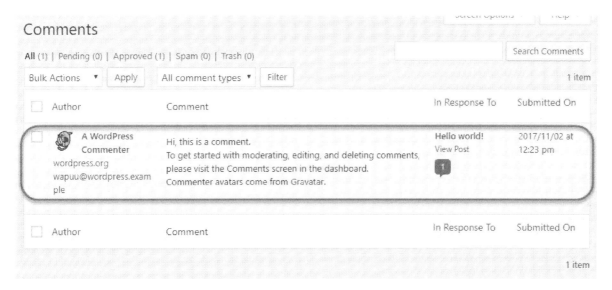

This screen looks like the last one. All the comments on the site are listed. At the moment, there is just the one that WordPress installed.

The **"In Response To"** column tells you where the comment was left. You can see that this comment was left in the Hello World post. You can click on the "Hello World" title to be taken to that post, open in the edit post screen.

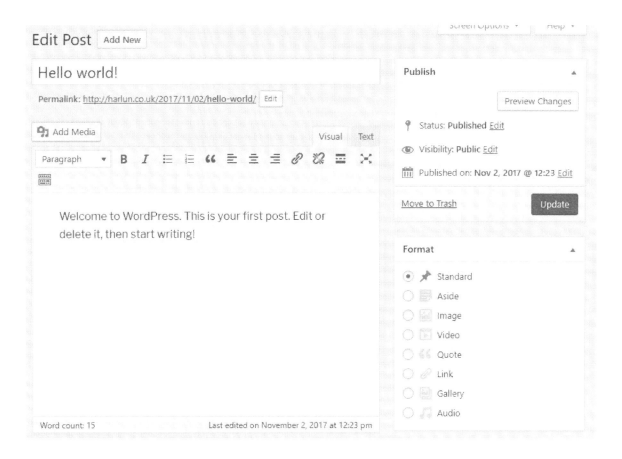

Deleting the Demo Post & Comment

To delete a post, click on **All Posts** inside the **Posts** menu in the dashboard sidebar.

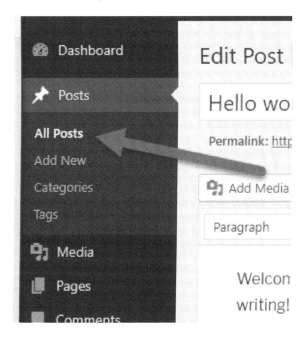

You'll see a list of all posts on the site. Find the one you want to delete, and move your mouse over the title:

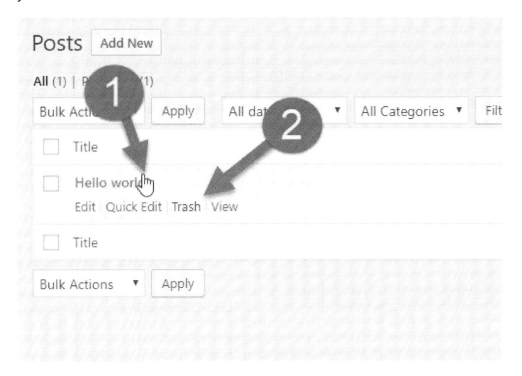

You'll see a menu that offers a **Trash** link. Click it. Once deleted, you'll see that your list of posts now shows (1) in Trash:

If you click the **Trash (1)** link, you'll open the trash:

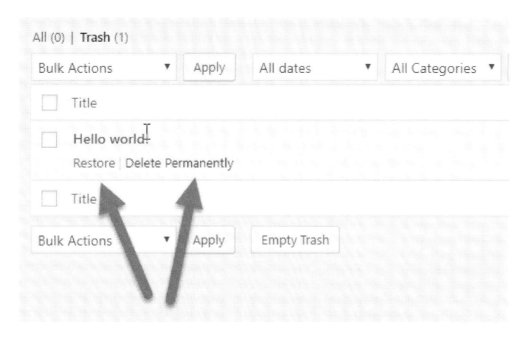

The trash contains all posts you've deleted (assuming you haven't emptied the trash), so you can see the Hello World post. The trash acts as a safety net. If you decide you want to restore a post you've deleted, you can. Or you can delete permanently.

There is another way to delete posts. To demonstrate this, I'll restore the Hello World post from the trash by clicking the **Restore** link.

Once restored, go back to the "All Posts" list again. There is the post, back from trash.

Check the box next to the post(s) you want to delete and select **Move to Trash** from the drop-down box.

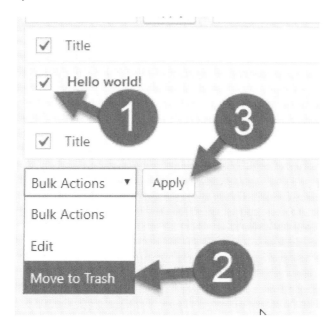

Then click the **Apply** button to move the selected posts to the trash.

This method of deleting posts is useful if you want to delete several posts. A similar system works in the comments section. You can delete comments one by one, or select several comments and send them all to the Trash in one go.

OK, now let's look at the Page that WordPress installed. Click the Pages menu item in the left sidebar.

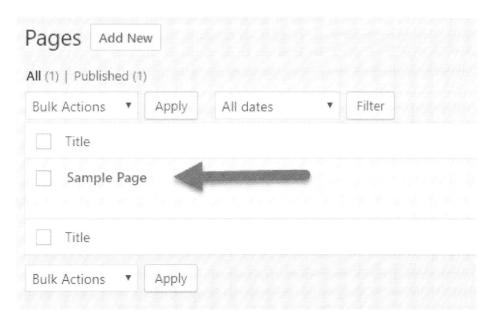

It's a familiar looking screen, isn't it? It's very similar to the screen for posts and for comments.

Click the **Sample Page** title to open the page in the Page editor.

You'll see that the main editor window is identical to the one for posts, though other options on the screen are different. We'll look at those later. Click the back button on your browser to go back to the "all pages" list.

Delete the Page in the same way you deleted the "Hello World!" post. The page will go to the page trash, which you can go into if you need to restore a page.

OK, we've deleted the post, which also deleted the comment associated with the post. We've also deleted the page. Therefore, the site is now empty:

POSTS

NOTHING FOUND

Ready to publish your first post? Get started here.

You have an empty site, now you need to add your content.

Planning the site

We've got a skeleton site, with no content. The first thing I suggest you do is to plan out what you want to include on your site. What content do you want to publish there?

You don't have to decide on everything just yet, but having a good plan before you start will make things a lot easier.

WordPress is so flexible that you can use it to create just about any type of website.

For example, let's consider this basic model for a site about WordPress:

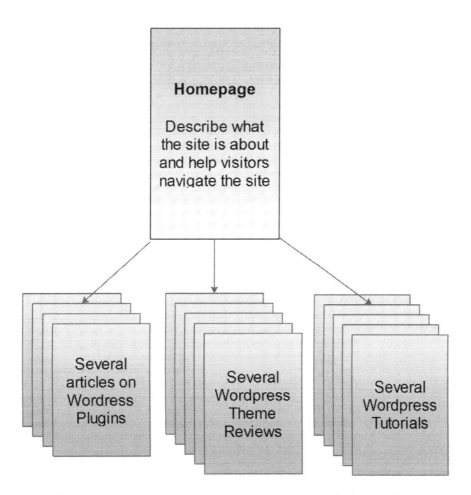

The homepage will introduce the site to my visitors and tell them what the site is about. The homepage will also help my visitors find what they are looking for. The site will have three main sections (for now, at least, but this may increase over time). There will be a section with several articles on WordPress plugins, another section with articles on WordPress themes, and then some WordPress tutorials.

In addition to this website "content", here are a few other things you need:

1. About Us page (for the visitors, and Google likes to see one).
2. Contact Us form (for the visitors and Google likes to see one)
3. Privacy Policy (for a little legal coverage)
4. Terms of Use (for a little legal coverage).

From the above, we can see that there are two distinct types of content.

There are those articles that we are writing to engage our visitors on the topic of our site, in this case, WordPress. These articles can typically and conveniently be grouped into "categories" and we will call this type of article **"website content"**.

The other type of content is the stuff that is not directly related to the topic of the site but is required to make the site complete and more professional (as well as provide ourselves with a little legal protection). This type of content is what I call the "legal pages". These "legal" pages are typically very similar for all sites you build, irrespective of topic.

This is where the difference between WordPress posts and WordPress pages should start to become obvious.

"Website content" is created as WordPress "posts".

"Legal pages" are created as WordPress "pages".

We'll look at this in more detail, but before we do, there are a few WordPress settings we need to change.

Getting the House in Order

WordPress comes installed with a number of default settings that really aren't in our best interests. In this section, we will make some changes and set up a few things. We are getting our house in order, ready for the first content.

WordPress Settings

I won't cover all the settings in WordPress, just the ones that are important at this stage. Follow along and make the changes as we go through them.

Checkpoint #1 – Author Profile

From the Users menu in the left sidebar, select **Your Profile**.

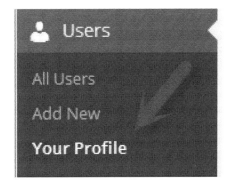

At the top of the screen, you'll see some personal options:

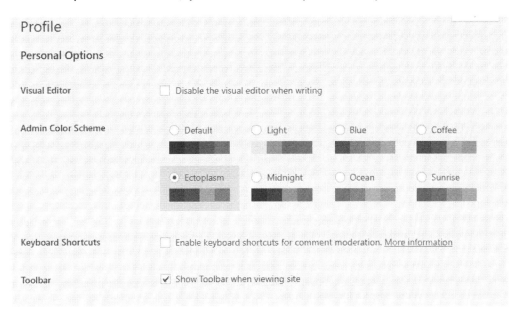

Make sure the "Disable the visual editor when writing" option is unchecked. Checking this option would remove the WYSIWYG editor from WordPress making it more difficult to create nicely formatted content.

The admin color scheme is a personal taste thing, so play around with the colors if you wish.

The "Show Toolbar when viewing site" should also be checked. This will place an admin bar across the top of your browser window when you are viewing your site while logged into your Dashboard. This admin bar gives you quick access to several dashboard features.

Underneath, you need to enter a few personal details.

Name

Username	andy	*Usernames cannot be changed.*
First Name	Andy	
Last Name	Williams	
Nickname *(required)*	Andy	
Display name publicly as	Andy ▾	

Contact Info

Email *(required)*	webmaster@ezseonews.com
Website	http://ezseonews.com

You cannot edit the username, so that box is greyed out.

Enter your first and last name.

In the Nickname, enter whatever you like. It will be prefilled with your username, but you can change it.

In the **Display name publicly as**, select the way you want your name appearing on the website. The options available will include combinations of your first and last name, nickname, username etc.

Make sure you have a valid email address in the contact info box.

Finally, on this screen, add a little information about yourself in the **Biographical Info** box.

This information may be used on your website, e.g. as an author bio after posts (depending on the theme):

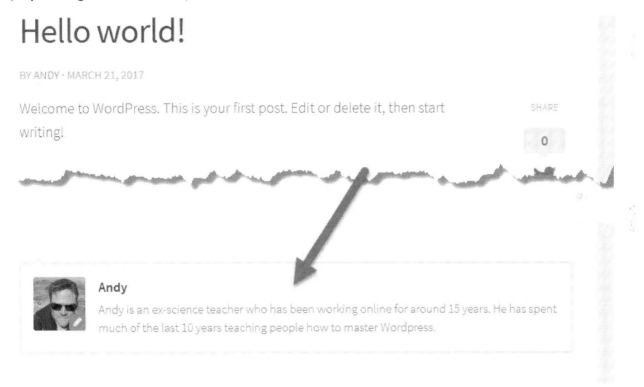

It may also be used as an introduction to your author page (a page that WordPress creates to highlight all content you, as an author, have written on the site).

Incidentally, if you want to find your own author page, visit a "post page" and look for your author name under the title:

UNCATEGORIZED

Hello world!

BY ANDY · MARCH 21, 2017

Welcome to WordPress. This is your first post. Edit or delete it, then start writing!

Not all themes will show this, but if it does show your "display name", click it to be taken to your author page.

Checkpoint #2 – Update Services

Go to **Writing** in the **Settings** menu in the left sidebar.

You will see a large box labeled **Update Services** (also referred to as a ping list). At the moment, there is just one entry.

Update Services

When you publish a new post, WordPress automaticall with line breaks.

http://rpc.pingomatic.com/

Save Changes

Essentially, whenever you post new content (or update an existing article) on your site, each of the sites listed in the update service list will be notified. This can mean your content gets indexed and included in the search engines within minutes. However, we can do better than just one update service.

Do a Google search for **WordPress update services + current year**, and find a list someone else has put together.

Copy and paste the list (as plain text) into your own "ping list", and save.

Each URL in the list needs to be on a separate line.

Checkpoint #3 – Reading Settings

Go to **Reading** in the **Settings** menu in the left sidebar:

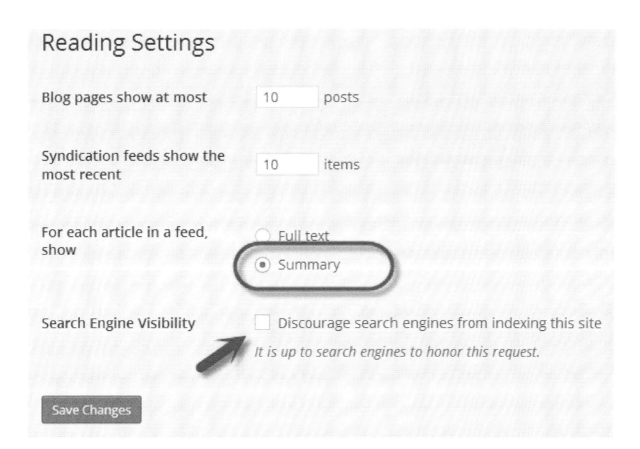

Make sure that **Summary** is selected, and that the search engine visibility box is UNCHECKED. If you check this option, the search engines WILL NOT index your pages or include them in the search engines. This can be useful if you don't want your site showing up in the search engines until you are ready, but I advise you to leave it unchecked. Google will come and see the site being actively developed, and this will encourage Google to come back frequently to spider and index your content.

Checkpoint #4 – Discussion Settings

Go to **Discussion** in the **Settings** menu in the left sidebar.

Most of these options can be left as they are. The ones to change are listed below:

Change 1:

Uncheck the option above, to help prevent spammy "comments" on your site.

Change 2:

Check the option to manually approve all comments.

Change 3:

The comment blacklist will help sort out a lot of spam comments before you even see them. You simply enter all the words you want to be considered spam, and if those words appear in a comment, the comment is marked as spam and sent to the spam folder.

You don't have to think of the words yourself as others have created lists for us. Do a Google search for **WordPress comment blacklist**. Find a list you can copy and paste into your own comment blacklist.

Change 4:

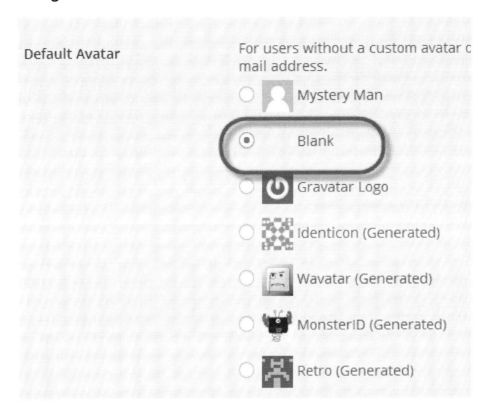

Under the default Avatar section, select **Blank**.

Reason: If someone leaving a comment does not have a Gravatar set up (this is an image associated with their email address), then we don't want an image displayed with their comment.

You can set it up to use any of those other images as the default image, but by using an image, you are slowing down the load times of your web pages. Imagine having 100 comments on a post, with 90 people not using a Gravatar. That would be 90 "default" images that need to load. Best save images for those times when people have bothered with the Gravatar, so select Blank, and an image will only appear when there is a valid Gravatar attached to the commenter's email address.

Checkpoint #5 – Permalinks

Under the **Settings** menu, go to **Permalinks**.

This is an important one.

The permalink structure will determine how the URLs of your site look when a page loads in a web browser.

For example, if you have the "plain" option selected, the URL for the Hello World post will look something like this:

P is the number of the post in the WordPress database. As this is the first post, the **post ID** of "hello world" is 1. That URL doesn't offer much to a visitor or search engine.

From a search engine point of view, it is far better to be more descriptive with your URLs. What I recommend you do is add the category and post name to the URL. Don't worry what that means right now, just make the following change:

Select **Custom Structure**, and enter:

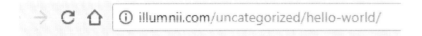

Save your changes.

To give you an idea of what this has done, look at the URL of the hello world post now:

illumnii.com/uncategorized/hello-world/

The word "Uncategorized" in the URL is the category of the "Hello World" post, which is currently called "Uncategorized" (the default category installed by WordPress). Of course, when we come to add content to our site, we will give our categories meaningful names.

Checkpoint #6 – Plugins

Click on the Plugins menu in the left sidebar. There will be a few plugins that were installed with WordPress.

The first is Akismet Anti-Spam.

	Plugin	Description
☐	Akismet Anti-Spam Activate | Edit | Delete	Used by millions, Akismet is quite possibly the best way in the world to while you sleep. To get started: activate the Akismet plugin and then g Version 4.0.1 | By Automattic | View details
☐	Hello Dolly Activate | Edit | Delete	This is not just a plugin, it symbolizes the hope and enthusiasm of an e Louis Armstrong: Hello, Dolly. When activated you will randomly see a every page. Version 1.6 | By Matt Mullenweg | View details

Akismet is a plugin that helps prevent comment spam, and it is extremely effective at what it does. However, if your site is commercial in nature (you make any money from the site), then you need the paid version of this plugin. Akismet can only be used for free if your site is a personal, non-profit website. If that's you, then click the "Activate" link under the plugin to "turn it on", and then head on over to Akismet to setup your account. See the Akismet site for details on how to do this.

If you are not going to be using a plugin, you should delete it, since leaving unused plugins on your server can increase the security risk of your site. Old plugins can have vulnerabilities that hackers use, and if you have old and unused plugins with these vulnerabilities on your server, you are a target.

To delete a plugin, click the delete link under the plugin.

	Hello Dolly	This is not just a p
☐	Hello Dolly Activate | Edit | Delete	This is not just a p Louis Armstrong: page. Version 1.6 | By N

Hello Dolly can be deleted, as can Akismet if you are not using it.

Checkpoint #7 - Gravatars

We mentioned Gravatars earlier. They are images that we can associate with our email address. If you look at the top right of your Dashboard, you will see your name and a placeholder image where your photo could be. Here is mine:

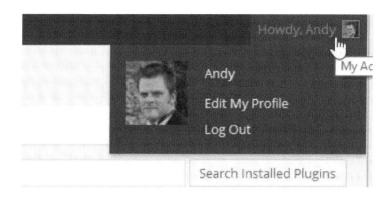

My photo is appearing there because I am using a Gravatar associated with my admin email address. If I use that email to post a comment on any other blog, my photo appears with my comment. Here is an example:

- high relevance to site theme

I had not thought about the nofollow link but now you've got me thinking.

I would appreciate your views on this
Many thanks & regards

Reply

Andy Williams **says**
17/3/2014 AT 08:25 (EDIT)

It's good to have a plan like this, and overall I like it, but I wou allow the following links on a Guest post.
1. Dofollow to Google Plus profile page. This would be dofol that authorship could be established. I don't know if anything changed, but when I tried several months ago, authorship wo work if the profile link was nofollow.

In the screenshot, I am replying to a comment. My Gravatar shows because I used my admin email when I commented.

Gravatars are a great way to brand yourself and I highly recommend you use a Gravatar for your own Admin email address. Visitors to your site love to know who they are dealing with, so get over your shyness and put your face on your site.

To sign up for a Gravatar, head on over to https://en.gravatar.com/

Look for the link to **Create your own Gravatar**, and follow the instructions. Now, whenever you post a comment on any website that is related to your own, use the email address that has your Gravatar attached, and your face will show up next to your comments on these other sites (unless they have Gravatars disabled, but very few do).

Checkpoint #8 - Adding a Sitemap

A sitemap is essentially a list of pages on your site, and it is used mainly by the search engines to find all your content. It is, therefore, a good idea to have one. The best way to add a sitemap is to use a plugin.

Click on **Add New** in the **Plugins** sidebar menu.

Search for **Yoast SEO** and find this plugin by Team Yoast:

Click the **Install Now.**

Once installed, click the **Activate** button that replaced the "install now" button.

You will now have a new sidebar menu:

As the menu title suggests, this plugin is more than a sitemap plugin. It's a very flexible and useful SEO plugin. It is beyond the scope of this book to teach you how to set this up, but I will show you how to activate the sitemap.

The first thing you need to do is activate some of the advanced features, so click on "dashboard" inside the SEO menu. This will take you to the General settings. Click on the "features" tab across the top:

.. and then click to enable the "Advanced Settings Pages". The default is disabled. Once done, scroll to the bottom of the page and click the "Save Changes" button.

Several new items will appear in the SEO menu:

Click on the XML Sitemaps item:

Make sure the XML sitemap functionality is "enabled" at the top, then scroll down and click "Save Changes".

That's it, your sitemap will now be created, and a link provided on the screen.

Click the link to be taken to your sitemap.

If you get a 404 error, meaning the page does not exist, make sure:

1. You have posts on your site that are published.
2. You have saved the permalink structure (even if you did not change it).

With a working sitemap, whenever you add a new post to your site it will automatically be added to this sitemap. Google and any other sites in your "ping list" will automatically be notified of the new content. You should find that once your site becomes established, new content will be indexed and found in Google within minutes of you clicking the "publish" button.

As we are getting close to adding content to the site, let's revisit posts and pages.

Pages v Posts

WordPress gives you two options for adding new content to your site. These are confusingly called "Pages" and "Posts".

Both use the exact same "What You See Is What You Get" (WYSIWYG) editor, making it easy to add content. However, you need to decide which one, and when, to use each.

I've already hinted at when to use pages and when to use posts earlier in this book, but I'd like to revisit this topic and explain the differences between pages and posts.

From now on, whenever I talk about posts, I am referring to WordPress POSTS, and whenever I talk about pages, I am referring to WordPress PAGES.

WordPress was originally designed with bloggers in mind, and WordPress "posts" were the tool given to the blogger so they could add updates to the blog. These WordPress posts were designed to be date-dependent so that posts could be listed in chronological order. Think of it much like a diary. Things happen and you enter them in the order they happen. If you then ordered the posts in date order, with the oldest posts at the top, you'd have a chronological list of posts over time. This was how posts were originally designed to be used.

So, what about WordPress "pages"?

Well, pages are not date-dependent. They are standalone pages and each page is usually unrelated to any other piece of content on the site. Remember I said that "legal" pages should be pages? Can you see why?

Post Categories

A major difference between posts and pages is that posts can be grouped and categorized (reinforcing the idea that posts can be related to other posts), whereas pages cannot (this isn't strictly true, but it helps if you think it is).

Remember the website structure I mapped out earlier for a site about WordPress?

There were a number of related articles about various WordPress plugins. There were also a bunch of related articles reviewing WordPress themes. The beauty of grouping and categorizing content on your site is that WordPress makes it easy to manipulate these groups of posts and treat them as a related whole.

For example, if a visitor lands on my review of the Thesis WordPress theme, doesn't it make sense to show that visitor a list of other theme reviews to give them more information before they choose one to buy?

WordPress makes this easy with posts, but there is no easy, built-in way of doing this with WordPress pages. Pages were designed to be separate, standalone pieces of content, unrelated to anything else on the site.

All posts are given a category, whereas pages are not. Earlier in this book, I showed you the URL of the "Hello World!" post after we made the change to the permalink structure.

The word "Uncategorized" in the URL is the category of the post.

Uncategorized is a default category that WordPress added when it was installed. We can, and will, change that later. However, think about my fictional website. The URLs of my theme reviews might look like this:

```
http://illumnii.com/themes/thesis
http://illumnii.com/themes/avada
http://illumnii.com/themes/genesis
http://illumnii.com/themes/customizr-pro
http://illumnii.com/themes/hueman
```

Some of my plugin reviews might look like this:

```
http://illumnii.com/plugins/yarpp
http://illumnii.com/plugins/related-posts
http://illumnii.com/plugins/yoast-seo
http://illumnii.com/plugins/akismet
http://illumnii.com/plugins/wp-dbmanager
```

.. and so on. You can instantly see that these groups of posts are related, because of the category in the URL.

This is a major SEO (Search Engine Optimization) benefit of posts as well. The search engines see these posts in the same category, and this helps them categorize and rank your content. The search engines know that these groups of posts are related, and carefully selected categories will help them categorize and rank your pages accordingly.

WordPress actually helps out even more.

For every category you create (I have two in the examples above – themes and plugins), WordPress creates a "Category page" that lists all posts in that category. Therefore, there will be a category page for themes and another for plugins. Their URLs will be as follows:

```
http://illumnii.com/category/plugins/
http://illumnii.com/category/themes/
```

The first category page will list all posts in the plugins category, and the second will list all posts in the themes category.

The search engines know that WordPress category pages list related posts, so it automatically knows that all posts listed on a category page have a common theme.

So, we can assign categories to posts. In fact, a post can be given more than one category. However, I don't recommend it. Categories are the top level of organization of posts, and I want you to stick to only using ONE category per post. What would a search engine "think" if a post was in two categories? It would probably wonder what the post was about, category 1 or category 2.

However, what if I had a category called "reviews"?

My "theme" posts could then go into both the themes category and the reviews category.

Similarly, my plugin reviews could go into the plugins category AND the reviews category.

If you have this dilemma, then you probably need to re-assess your category structure. However, WordPress does give us another tool that can help solve the problem.

Tags!

Post Tags

So, categories are the main way we categorize and group posts. WordPress also gives us a secondary method for categorizing content, called Tags. These are just words or phrases we can assign to a post, like keywords related to the post. So, we could "tag" all review posts as "reviews", while keeping them in tightly focused categories.

Just as WordPress creates a "category page" for all categories you define, it also creates a tag page for each tag you use. For example, if you tagged 5 of your posts with the tag "review", then WordPress would create a review tag page that lists those five posts.

http://illumnii.com/tag/review/

On the reviews tag page of my WordPress site, we would see posts from both the themes and plugins categories. Can you see the power of this? It's an extra level of organization!

A post can have multiple tags assigned to it, but only create tags if they are going to be used on multiple posts. Never use a tag that will only appear on one post.

The rule is that each post should only be in ONE category, but can have multiple tags.

Let me give you an example of when you might use a tag.

Suppose you have a site about vacuum cleaners. You have decided on categories like Dyson, Hoover, Eureka, Kirby, Dirt Devil and so on. In other words, you are using the manufacturer names as categories. All Dyson vacuum reviews go in the Dyson category, all Kirby reviews go in the Kirby category.

This makes sense because as webmaster, you decided that most visitors know the brand of vacuum they want, so grouping by brand helps them more easily find the model that suits them best. To find a Dyson, they can simply go to your Dyson category page where all Dyson reviews are listed.

However, sometimes a visitor does not know the brand of vacuum he wants. All they know is that they want a hand-held vacuum, or a canister vacuum, or maybe a vacuum designed to deal with pet hair.

This is where I would use tags.

I'd have the following tags:

Upright, canister, pets, hand-held, HEPA filter, etc.

Therefore, my Dyson DC31 Animal review would be put in the Dyson category, but I could tag it with pets and hand-held.

The beauty of tags is that we can manipulate them in the same way we do categories. If someone on your site is interested in a "hand-held vacuums", but not sure which manufacturer, you can show them a list of all vacuums "tagged" with "hand-held".

As mentioned earlier, WordPress creates a "tag page" for each tag you use. Each tag page lists all posts that have used that tag. So WordPress would create a page that lists all "hand-held" vacuum reviews.

Sound familiar? Yes, it's very much like the category pages we mentioned earlier.

So, posts can have categories and tags assigned to them.

I do have a few rules on using categories and tags efficiently. These rules will keep you out of trouble. Here they are:

1. Only one category per post.
2. You can have multiple tags, but try to limit each post to 5 or fewer tags. The more tags you use in a post, the more spammy your site begins to look to Google.
3. Never use a tag if only one post will be tagged with it. I personally only create a tag if it will be used on a minimum of three posts. Tags, like categories, are there to help organize and group your posts. If there is only one post using a tag, it's not a group. Remember that WordPress creates a "tag page" for each tag you use. If you only have one post using a tag, then that tag page will basically just contain one post. That would be considered duplicate content by Google since you already have that one post on its own "post page", as well as on a category page.
4. Never create a tag with the same name as a category.

Tags are ultimately there to help you make your site better for your visitors. Don't abuse them.

Post Excerpts

Another great feature is post **excerpts.** When you enter a post, you have the option of entering an excerpt as well.

By default, WordPress hides the excerpt entry box on the edit post screen, so we need to unhide it. To hide and unhide various aspects of the Dashboard, WordPress has "Screen Options", which you can see in the top right of your dashboard.

The screen options you see at any point in the dashboard will be related to the section of the dashboard you are currently viewing. Therefore, since excerpts are related to posts, we need to be adding or editing a post to see the option.

Click on **Posts** in the sidebar menu. This will bring up a list of posts on your site. If you have one, click on the title of the post to open the editing screen. If you don't have one, click **Add New** (in the posts menu). This will create a post and open it for editing.

Now that you are on the post editing screen, click where it says "Screen Options" to open the menu:

Clicking that button will expand it:

As you can see, **Excerpt** is unchecked. If we check that box, the Edit post screen adds this new entry box:

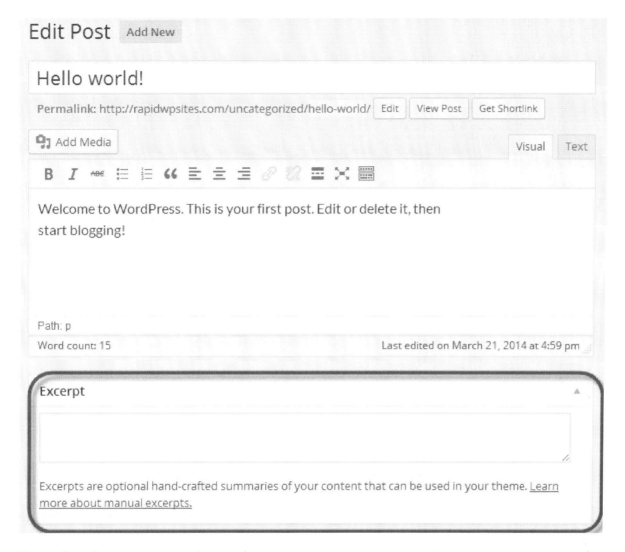

Now when I enter a post, I can also enter a separate excerpt.

Note that the "Screen Options" are dynamic, and will show you just the options that are relevant to the Dashboard screen you are viewing. In the screenshots above, I am in the Edit post screen, so the options I am given relate to the Edit posts screen.

OK, so let's go back to our discussion of excerpts, and look at what they are, and why we would use them.

An excerpt is a short summary or description of a post. Some WordPress themes and plugins can use the excerpt, for example, to show to visitors, or as a meta description of the post.

Let's see an example of an excerpt being used properly on a site. This screenshot shows the sidebar of a website that is using a plugin to display recent posts in a category:

Juicing recipes

Very Berry Sprouted Smoothie

Alfalfa sprouts are a product of alfalfa seeds. The tiny sprouts are thread-like in structure with green tops. The seeds can be cultivated anywhere on the planet irrespective of climate or temperature. The highly nutritive sprouts have a mild taste making them the ideal addition to any smoothie recipe.

Paleo Tomato Salad

Enthusiasts of paleo and primal diets love this recipe: Ingredients: 3 or 4 tomatoes Bacon lardons 2 boiled eggs A tablespoon of mayonnaise A few anchovies A tablespoon of olive oil. Directions: Combine the sliced tomatoes with peeled boiled eggs cut into squares in a large salad bowl. Fry the bacon, let it cool and [...]

Notice the top one. The description of the post is nicely defined and "complete". The one lower down, however, is not. Notice that the description for the second one ends with [...].

This plugin looks for an excerpt to use as the post description. If it finds an excerpt, it will use it. If it does not find one, it will use the first bit of text in the article and create a description from that. When it does that, you end up with a description that is not complete, copied from the start of the article, and ends with [...].

You can see how using excerpts makes your site look more professional, and better for your visitors. It also allows you to write some unique text that will act as a description to entice visitors. It's also better for the search engines because they see different content in the description, instead of just part of the first paragraph of the post.

Posts and RSS Feeds

Another important difference between posts and pages is that posts appear in RSS feeds, pages do not.

WordPress sites automatically create RSS feeds. These are special files that contain a list of the most recent posts on your site.

WordPress creates a single RSS feed for your entire site, but it also creates separate feeds for each category, each tag, all posts by a particular author, etc.

RSS feeds are important tools to notify people, and other websites, that you have published new content. Personally, I monitor the RSS feeds (using a free service over at Feedly.com) of my favorite websites, and when they post new content, the feed is updated (automatically by WordPress) and I get notified of that new content.

So, when do you use Posts, and when Pages?

The rule is simple.

Use Pages for your "legal pages" (remember those), and posts for "website content" (the articles you write to engage your visitors).

Note that WordPress is extremely flexible and you could create an entire site using just pages. Or, you could create a site that uses pages for "main articles", then posts as a type of blog attached to your site. However, I think that when you are just starting out with WordPress, you need to use the tools WordPress gives you in the way they were designed to be used, and that is what I am teaching you in this book.

Now you know the main differences between posts and pages, it's time to create some. However, before we do that, let's look at the editor we use to enter content.

Using the WYSIWYG Editor

Whether you are entering a post or a page, it all starts with the same WYSIWYG editor. You can see it if you go to **Add New** in the **Posts** menu in the left sidebar. Go on; add a new post so that you can use it as a test document to explore the editor.

The first thing to do is click that button on the far right of the toolbar.

That's better.

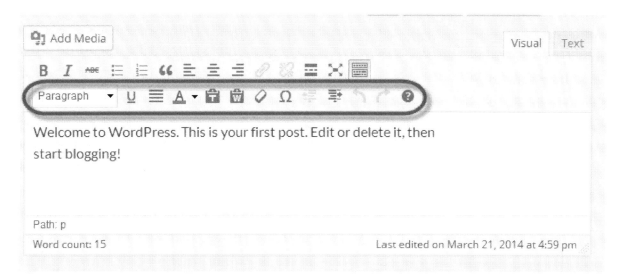

You now have another row of buttons to help you enter and format your article.

If you are familiar with a Word processor, you will intuitively know how to use this editor.

The large white area under the buttons is where you type text. Go on, try typing in the box. As you type, you will see that the editor automatically wraps text onto the next line when you get to the end of the line.

This brings me to an important tip. When you are typing text into this editor, never press the return key on your keyboard to try to force the text to wrap onto the next line. Let the editor wrap the text for you. Only press the return key ONCE at the end of a paragraph.

As you type, the editor box gets longer. Use the scroll bars if you need to navigate up or down your document.

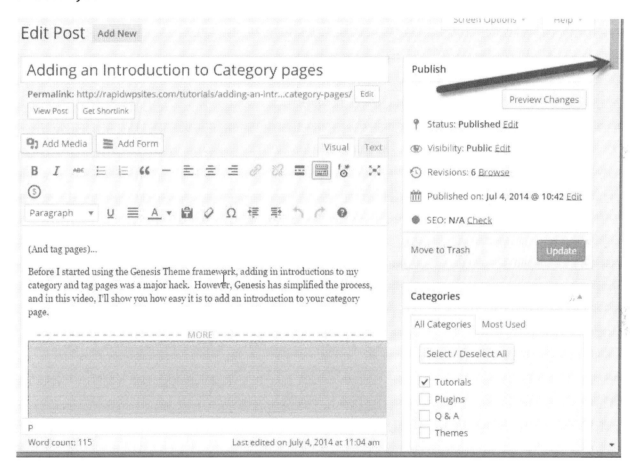

OK, you can see how easy it is to type plain text into the window.

Headlines in your document

The main headline on any post or page will be created by WordPress for you, from the text you type into the "Enter title here" box:

Go on, type in a title for your test document.

Add New Post

This is my test document

Permalink: http://rapidwpsites.com/uncategorized/7/ [Edit]

[📷] Add Media

B *I* ~~ABC~~ ☰ ☰ " ☰ ☰ ☰ 🔗 ✂ ☰ ✕ ▦

Paragraph ▾ U ☰ **A** ▾ 📋 📋 🧽 Ω ➡ ➡ ↶ ↷ ❓

This is a test post to see how the editor works. This is a test post to see how the editor works. This is a test post to see how the editor works. This is a test post to see how the editor works. I can see that it automatically wraps onto the next line when it gets to the end.

This is the second paragraph. This is a test post to see how the editor works. This is a test post to see how the editor works. This is a test post to see how the editor works. I can see that it automatically| wraps onto the next line when it gets to the end.

Over on the right of the editor screen, in the **Publish** options, you will see a **Preview** button. This button allows you to see what your post will look like when it is live on your site. Click **Preview** and your test post will open in a new browser tab:

THIS IS MY TEST DOCUMENT

🕐 MARCH 23, 2014   👤 ANDY   💬 LEAVE A COMMENT   ✏ EDIT

This is a test post to see how the editor works. This is a test post to see how the editor works. This is a test post to see how the editor works. This is a test post to see how the editor works. I can see that it automatically wraps onto the next line when it gets to the end.

This is the second paragraph. This is a test post to see how the editor works. This is a test post to see how the editor works. This is a test post to see how the editor works. I can see that it automatically wraps onto the next line when it gets to the end.

As you can see, the post title is there above the content of my post.

It is always a good idea to add sub-headers, bullets and other formatting to make your posts look better for the visitor. Let's add a sub-headline before the second paragraph.

Back in the editor, position your mouse where you want the sub-headline to appear and left click your mouse to set the editing position.

NOTE: You won't be able to set the cursor in the white space between the paragraphs, so just click at the very start of the second paragraph.

This is a test post to see how the editor works. This is a test post to see how the editor works. This is a test post to see how the editor works. This is a test post to see how the editor works. I can see that it automatically wraps onto the next line when it gets to the end.

This is the second paragraph. This is a test post to see how the editor works. This is a test post to see how the editor works. This is a test post to see how the editor works. I can see that it automatically wraps onto the next line when it gets to the end.

You will see a blinking cursor which marks the point you selected. This "edit cursor" (as we will call it from now on) is a short, thin, vertical line, and it marks the position that text will appear if you type.

Since we want to type a sub-headline at this point, just start typing the headline,

see how the editor works. This is a test post to see how the editor works. This is a test post to see how the editor works. I can see that it automatically wraps onto the next line when it gets to the end.

Adding a sub-headlineThis is the second paragraph. This is a test post to see how the editor works. This is a test post to see how the editor works. This is a test post to see how the editor works. I can see that it automatically wraps onto the next line when it gets to the end.

.. and when you finish the headline, press the return key.

This is a test post to see how the editor works. This is a test post to see how the editor works. This is a test post to see how the editor works. This is a test post to see how the editor works. I can see that it automatically wraps onto the next line when it gets to the end.

Adding a sub-headline

This is the second paragraph. This is a test post to see how the editor works. This is a test post to see how the editor works. This is a test post to see how the editor works. I can see that it automatically wraps onto the next line when it gets to the end.

OK, we now have the headline on its own line. If you preview the post again, you will see it is normal text and does not look like a headline. We need to format it.

Using your mouse, select the headline. You can do this by clicking at the start of the headline, holding the click, and dragging your mouse to the end of the headline. When selected, the headline is highlighted.

This is a test post to see how the editor works. This is a test post to see how the editor works. This is a test post to see how the editor works. This is a test post to see how the editor works. I can see that it automatically wraps onto the next line when it gets to the end.

Adding a sub-headline

This is the second paragraph. This is a test post to see how the editor works. This is a test post to see how the editor works. This is a test post to see how the editor works. I can see that it automatically wraps onto the next line when it gets to the end.

OK, with the headline selected, we need to choose the headline style to use. In the editor toolbar, you can see a drop-down box that currently says "Paragraph". This is on the second row of buttons, and you may not see this row if you didn't click the top right toolbar button earlier (in which case, do that now).

Click where you see the word "Paragraph" and the drop-down box opens, giving you options.

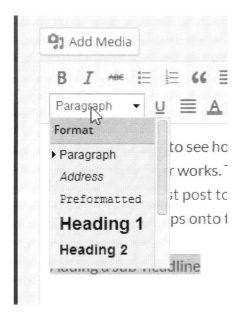

You can see Heading 1 and Heading 2 at the bottom. If you scroll down that box, you will see other headline options as well.

When WordPress creates the post, the headline at the top of the page (which we saw earlier) is set as Heading 1. This is the largest headline.

You should only ever have ONE Heading 1 per post/page.

Sub-headings should, therefore, be Heading 2, and if you have sub-headings inside a Heading 2 section, these should be Heading 3, and so on.

OK, select Heading 2 from the list, and your headline will change formatting in the editor.

This is a test post to see how the editor works. This is a test post to see how the editor works. This is a test post to see how the editor works. This is a test post to see how the editor works. I can see that it automatically wraps onto the next line when it gets to the end.

Adding a sub-headline

This is the second paragraph. This is a test post to see how the editor works. This is a test post to see how the editor works. This is a test post to see how the editor works. I can see that it automatically wraps onto the next line when it gets to the end.

If you accidentally select the wrong formatting, just highlight the headline again, and reselect.

To change the formatting of any text in the editor, you follow the same routine. Select the text you want to format, and then select the formatting option in the toolbar.

Try it with bold and italic text. Select a bit of text in your test post, then click the Bold and/or Italic button in the toolbar.

Other useful formatting options on the top row of the toolbar include the list buttons. There are bullet lists and numbered lists:

To create a bullet list, type the first item you want in your list on its own line in the editor, just like you did when entering the sub-heading.

see how the editor works. This is a test post to see how th
works. This is a test post to see how the editor works. I c
automatically wraps onto the next line when it gets to th

this is item one in my list|

Adding a sub-headline

This is the second paragraph. This is a test post to see ho
works. *This is a test post to see how the editor works*. This i
to see how the editor works. I can see that it automatica
onto the next line when it gets to the end.

Path: p

You do not have to select that line of text to create a bullet point. Simply click so that the edit cursor is somewhere on the line. Now click the bullet button. The line will become a bullet point. Clicking the bullet button again will toggle the bullets off/on. This can be useful if you end up with a bullet point at the end of your list:

works. This is a test post to see hov
automatically wraps onto the next

- this is item one in my list
- this is the second item
- this is the third I
-

Adding a sub-headline

Just move your edit cursor to that line, and press the bullet button to toggle bullets off for that line.

To add another bullet point to the list, move the edit cursor to the end of the first bullet point, and press the return key on your keyboard. A second bullet point appears, ready for typing in the next item in the list.

When you get to the end of your bullet list, you can simply move the edit cursor away from the list, and carry on working on other areas of your document.

On the top toolbar, you also have options for aligning your paragraphs. Typically, you won't want to change this, but the options are there to center and right align if you need them.

One of the more important formatting options in the top toolbar is the ability to add hyperlinks in your content. A hyperlink is simply a link to another web page.

To add a hyperlink, highlight the text you want to use as the link text, and then click the **Insert/Edit link** button.

: how the editor works. This is a test post to
 ‹s. This is a test post to see how the editor
 t to see how the editor works. I can see that
  onto the next line when it gets to the end.

 ‹ list

A popup will appear where you can enter the details of the link. The link text will be highlighted:

Enter the URL of the page you want to link to in the box.

If you want this link to open in a new browser tab when someone clicks on it, then click on the cog at the far right of this popup:

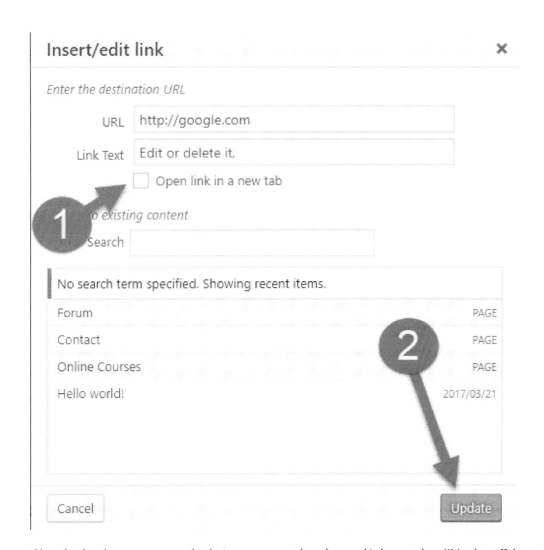

Check the box to open link in a new tab, then click on the "Update" button.

The link will be updated in the editor.

If you want to link to another page on your site, you can use the built-in page selector. Highlight the text you want to use in the link, and click on the link button in the toolbar:

Now click the cog, and in the window that appears, you can select the page or post you want to link to:

Insert/edit link   ✕

Enter the destination URL

URL

Link Text   Welcome

            ✔ Open link in a new tab

Or link to existing content

Search

No search term specified. Showing recent items.

Forum	PAGE
Contact	PAGE
Online Courses	PAGE
Hello world!	2017/03/21

Cancel   Add Link

Just click on the page (note there is a search box to help find pages as your site gets bigger), and then click the **Add Link** button. This will then update the editor with the new link to that page.

To remove a link in your post, click somewhere in the link to place the edit cursor inside the link text. Now click the **Unlink** button in the toolbar (it's right next to the insert/edit link button).

your first post. Edit or delete it, ther

The final option I want to cover on the top row of the toolbar is the **Insert More Tag** button. This is used to insert a break in your post, to stop any further text from appearing. This break will be obeyed by WordPress on all web pages where the post appears, EXCEPT the actual post page. Therefore, the more tag is obeyed on the homepage, category pages, tag pages, author pages etc. When WordPress find a "more tag", it truncates your post at that point, offering the visitor a "more" link to read the rest of the post.

OK, let's try this.

Insert a "More tag" after your first paragraph. You can do this by placing the cursor at the end of the paragraph and clicking the "more tag" button. In the editor, you will see the more tag has been added:

If you preview the post, you won't notice any difference, since the preview is showing you the "post page", and this is the only page where the more tag is ignored. To see the more tag in action, click the **Publish** button:

This makes the post live on your site. If you now visit the homepage of your site (assuming you haven't jumped ahead in the book and made the homepage show a static page), you'll see your test post is now truncated where you added the more tag. You can also see this on the category page of the post:

CATEGORY: UNCATEGORIZED

MARCH 21, 2017 EDIT

Hello world!

Lorem ipsum dolor sit amet, consectetur adipiscing elit. Maecenas volutpat, diam vel tempor molestie, diam massa gravida libero, ac blandit risus libero id dolor. Quisque lectus neque, bibendum ut fringilla id, pretium a nunc. Cras malesuada felis vel aliquam hendrerit. Morbi sit amet consequat lectus, ac ornare risus.

Continue reading

Notice that WordPress is offering you a link to "Continue reading".

Clicking that opens the full post page, with the screen scrolled down to the position of the more tag, so your visitor can carry on reading the post. Go on, click the "Continue reading" link to understand how this all works.

On the bottom row of the toolbar, there are a couple of options I want to tell you about. The first one is the clipboard with the "T" inside. If you click this button, it stays selected. You have just turned plain text paste mode on. If you are copying and pasting from a rich text format, e.g. Word, then turn on plain text pasting so that formatting is stripped out. When you paste from Word, only the text is copied across.

The only other toolbar buttons I want to mention are the redo/undo buttons:

You are probably already familiar with undo and redo features of your Word processor. If you do something wrong, you can click the undo button to undo it. If you undo something and need to redo it, click the redo button.

The Visual / Text editors

You may have noticed two tabs at the top right of the editor - "Visual" and "Text".

The visual editor is selected at the moment, and with the visual editor, we can design our content visually using the WYSIWYG editor and formatting buttons.

Click on the Text tab, and you'll see the contents of your post as HTML code.

You are unlikely to need to modify the HTML code directly, so I won't discuss the Text editing screen and its options. Just know it's there.

Inserting Media into your post

Media can be images, video or sound files. You insert them the same way in each case, by using the Media Library.

To insert an image, move your edit cursor to the position of your document where you want to insert the image.

Now click the **Add Media** button.

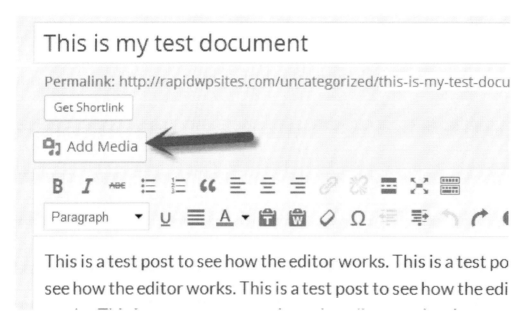

The **Add Media** screen opens, with two tabs.

1. Upload Files

2. Media Library

On the Upload files tab, you can add new media files to the Media library. In fact, you can drag and drop any media files from your computer to this screen.

Drop files anywhere to upload

Select Files

Maximum upload file size: 8MB.

If you prefer, you can also select the files from your computer by clicking the **Select Files** button. Both options will add the files to your media library.

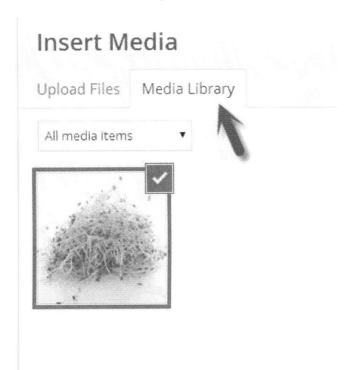

Insert Media

Upload Files   Media Library

All media items ▼

On the Media Library tab, you can select any of the images you have added to your library, and insert them into your post. When you click on an image, you will see an **Attachment Details** panel open on the right-hand side of the screen.

This panel lets you edit "features" of the image that is currently selected. At the top, you can see the image size and dimensions:

wordpress-seo.png
May 11, 2017
111 KB
756 × 168
Edit Image
Delete Permanently

The **Edit Image** link will allow you to do some basic image editing, like rotating the image, changing the dimensions, etc.

Under those options, you have the URL (of the image), Title, Caption, Alt Text, and description of the image. You can edit these. For example, the ALT text can be set here, and that will then be used when displaying the image to the visually impaired.

At the bottom of the attachment details, you can set the default alignment and size, as well as choosing where the media file links to. For example, you might like to make your images clickable to open the attachment page, media file, or link to a custom page (your image might be a "Buy Now" button). Alternatively, if you don't want the image clickable, you can choose **None** in the **Link To** box.

Most of these options can also be changed once an image is inserted into a post, so you don't need to make all necessary settings here.

To insert an image into a post, click on the **Insert into Post** button at the bottom of the attachment details panel.

I recommend you set the alignment to either right or left, as this will make the text of your post flow around the image.

Adding a sub-headline

This is the second paragraph. This is a test post to see how the editor works. *This is a test post to see how the editor works.* This is a test post to see how the editor works. I can see that it automatically wraps onto the next line when it gets to the end.

There is another way to add images to posts.

When WordPress 3.9 was released, it gave us the option of dragging and dropping an image from our computer, directly into the post.

Find the file on your computer that you want to add to your post, click and hold the mouse button, and drag the image into your post. As your mouse goes over the post, you'll see the screen change:

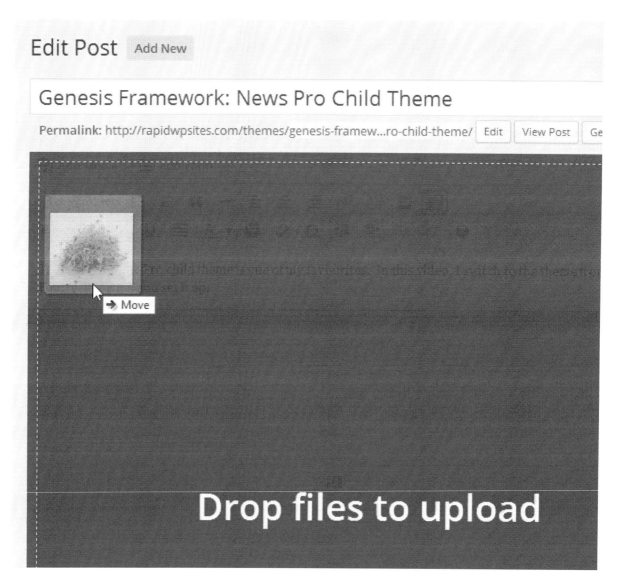

You can now drop the image into the post. When you do, WordPress will upload the image to your media library.

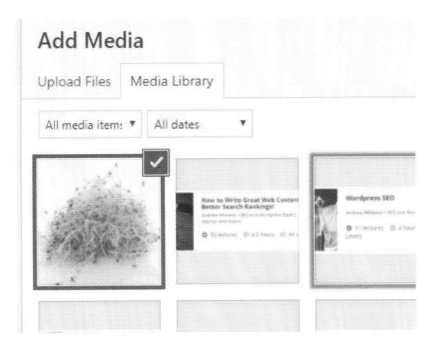

Add Media

You can see the image I just dropped top left.

Click the **Insert into post** button to insert the image into your post.

Once inserted, you can drag and move your image around the post to put it in the correct location, as well as set alignment, resize (click the image to see the options available) and edit/delete the caption.

Nulla ac malesuada nulla, vel pharetra dolor. Duis semper rutrum urna. Phase dignissim, vel luctus diam commodo. Phasellus non augue eu ante lobortis tir.

Adding a YouTube Video

If you want to add a video from a video sharing site, like YouTube, that's easy.

Find the video on YouTube and grab the URL of the video.

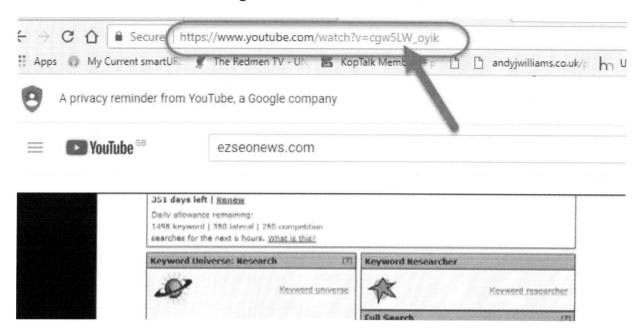

In the WYSIWYG editor, move your mouse to the position you want to insert the video and insert the URL. Give it a few seconds, and you should find that the video will appear, right there in your post.

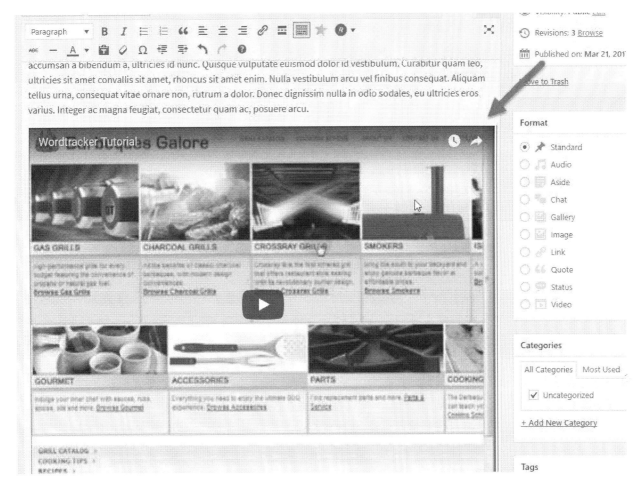

You can even click on the play button while you are editing your post, and the video will play.

OK, you have all the tools you need to create content for your site. Let's create some web pages.

Creating Pages – About, contact & terms

The first web pages we are going to create on the site are the ones I call "legal" pages. Remember? We talked about them earlier. These are the web pages that are not specifically written to engage our visitors but are required to make the site complete, and more professional.

Let's start with the Contact page. This will allow your visitors to contact you by filling out a form on your site. For this, we are going to use a plugin.

Click **Add New** in the Plugins sidebar menu.

In the search box, type **contact form 7**

You should see this plugin:

Click the **Install Now** button. The plugin will install, and the button will change to **Activate**. Click to **Activate** the plugin.

You will now have a new menu in the sidebar, labeled **Contact**.

Under the Contact menu, click **Contact Forms**.

The plugin installed a demo form for you, and that serves our purpose.

Highlight the **shortcode** for the form and copy it.

We now need to create a Page that can host the contact form. Under the **Pages** menu, click **Add New.**

For the title, type **Contact** or **Contact Us.**

In the WYSIWYG editor, paste the contact form shortcode.

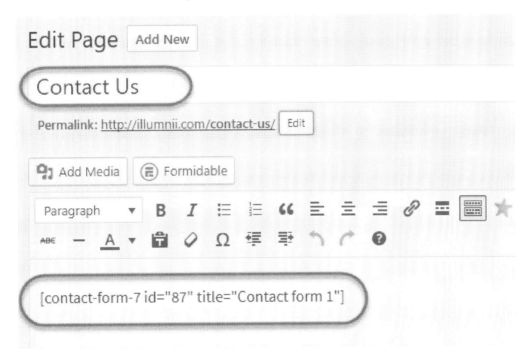

Click the **Publish** button to publish the page.

With the page published, click on the **Permalink** to the page:

The new contact page will open. Note that this is an easy way to visit any post or page on your site, directly from the editor, after it is published.

You will see your contact form on the page. If you fill it in and send a test message, you should receive it at the email address you entered as your admin email when you set WordPress up.

At the bottom of the contact form, do you see a comments section? Chances are you won't but it does depend on how WordPress is set up.

If you do, that is something you really need to turn off on the contact page, since comments should be restricted to web pages where you want discussion and feedback on your content (i.e. the posts). We don't want comments at the bottom of the contact page!

To turn comments off for the contact form (or any page where they are enabled), open the page edit screen for the contact page.

In the Screen Options top right, make sure **Discussion** is checked:

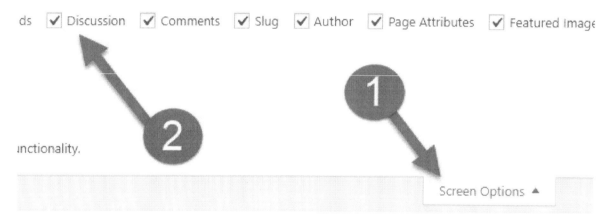

This will make the discussion section visible on the Edit Page screen:

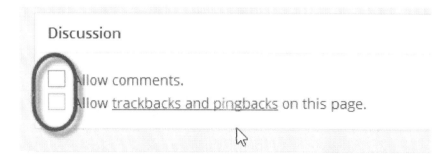

Uncheck both boxes to prevent comments and trackbacks/pingbacks.

You can now re-publish your page.

If you have already published the page, the "Publish" button is now labeled **Update**.

Once updated, go back to your contact page and you should find the comment form has gone.

That's the first page complete.

OK, now for the "About Us" page. This is where you have a chance to write a little bit about yourself and your site, so your visitors know about the person/company behind the site. The "About Us" page is often the most visited page on many websites, so bear that in mind.

Click **Add New** from the **Pages** sidebar menu.

This will start a new page.

For the title, use something simple, like "About", "About Me" or "About Us".

In the WYSIWYG editor, write the contents of your "About" page.

What should you include?

That is your choice, but here are some things I try to include in mine:

1. I like to begin by stating the goal of my website, but usually approach this from the point of view of the visitors. What are their problems or interests and how can my site help them.
2. Add your name and photo.
3. Add a bit of information about yourself.
4. Break up the page with bullet points and sub-headings to make it easier to read or scan.

5. Include your contact details or a link to your contact form. Note you can paste the contact form shortcode at the bottom of your about page to include it there as well if you want.

Once you have entered the text for your About page, click the **Publish** button to make it live on your site.

Visit your own about page.

You may find the comment form at the bottom of the page, so go in and turn it off if you need to.

The final pages we want to create are as follows:

1. Privacy Policy
2. Terms of Use
3. Possibly a Disclaimer depending on the type of stuff you have on your site.

While you can create these pages manually and add your own legal documents, I prefer to get them up quickly using another plugin.

The plugin I use is called "Auto Terms of Service and Privacy. Go to **Plugins**, **Add New** and search for it.

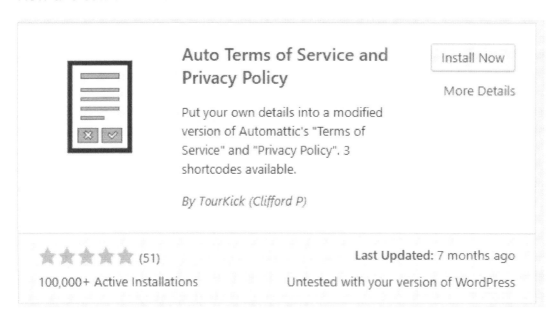

This one only creates the Terms and the Privacy policy, but that is enough to get you up and running.

Install and activate the plugin.

Click on **Auto TOS & PP** in the **Settings** menu.

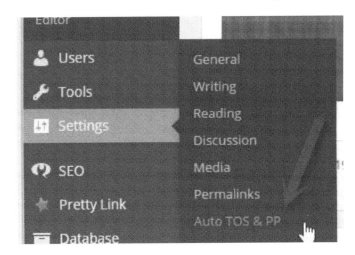

There is a form on this screen that you need to fill. It's fairly intuitive, so go ahead and fill it in.

Once you've filled that, change the top **On/Off** switch to **On / Displaying**:

Once done, click on the Save button at the bottom. If you have missed any required fields, the on/off switch won't change to **On / Displaying**, so check your form if you have issues.

We need to create some pages, but don't close this screen as we'll need the shortcodes.

Auto Terms of Service and Privacy Policy Options

Settings

Available shortcodes:

[my_terms_of_service_and_privacy_policy]

[my_terms_of_service]

[my_privacy_policy]

Under the **Pages** menu in the sidebar, right-click **Add New** and select to open in a new tab.

Enter the title "Privacy Policy". In the WYSIWYG editor, paste in the shortcode for the privacy policy:

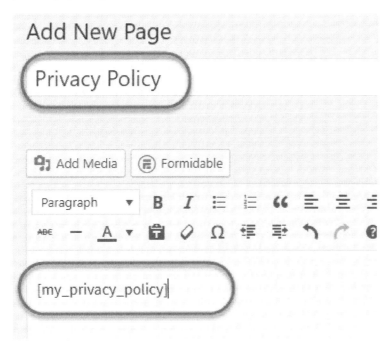

Now click the **Publish** button on the right.

Once the page is published, open the page in your browser (using the permalink) to see your new Privacy Policy.

Repeat this process, adding a page for the Terms of Service (call the page title "Terms").

OK; with that completed, you now have a Privacy Policy and Terms of Service page created. If you need a disclaimer, you'll need to manually create that.   Just create a WordPress Page, and add the disclaimer to the WYSIWYG editor. If you need help with your disclaimer, search Google for "sample disclaimer". Depending on the type of site you run, you might need a medical disclaimer, outbound links disclaimer, etc.

If necessary, turn off comments on these pages.

Top Navigation Menu

To make it easy for site visitors to find the legal pages, we need to create a custom menu. Let's do that now.

Under the **Appearance** menu in the left sidebar, select **Menus**.

At the top, click the link to create a new menu:

You will now be able to enter a name for your menu:

I call this menu my "legal menu". Always give menus a descriptive name so you know what they are, simply by looking at the title.

Next, click the **Create Menu** button.

This creates an empty menu that we can add items to.

On the left, you'll see a list of your pages:

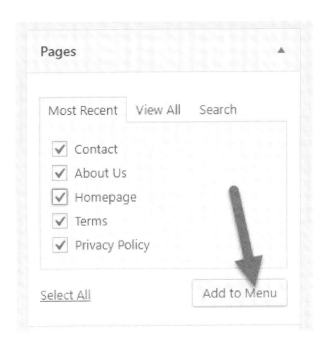

Place a checkmark next to the pages you want to be included in your menu. I've checked:

- Contact
- About Us
- Homepage
- Privacy Policy
- Terms of Use

This menu will link to all the important pages.

Once checked, click the **Add to Menu** button.

You will now see your list of pages in a column on the right. You can click and drag these pages so that they are in the order you want them to appear on your site.

You can also nest menu items, like this:

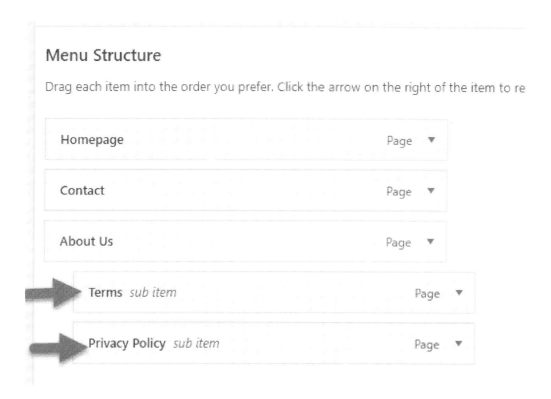

Menu Structure

Drag each item into the order you prefer. Click the arrow on the right of the item to re

Homepage	Page ▼
Contact	Page ▼
About Us	Page ▼
Terms *sub item*	Page ▼
Privacy Policy *sub item*	Page ▼

See how the Privacy Policy and the Terms of Use are indented under the "parent" About Us page?

When you indent pages in a menu, only the parent pages show in the menu on your site, but when a visitor moves their mouse over the parent page, a drop-down menu appears showing the indented pages.

Here it this menu on my site.

Homepage   Contact   About Us ⌄

.. and if I mouse-over the Disclaimer menu item:

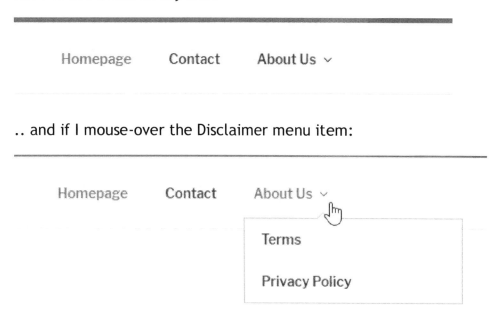

Homepage   Contact   About Us ⌄

Terms

Privacy Policy

The exact look of this will depend on the theme you are using.

In my case, I don't want the privacy and terms nested under the About Us page, so I'll remove the indent from my menu. However, this type of nesting of menu items is useful to stop your menu becoming too big.

To display your menu on your website, you need to tell your "theme", where to put it.

At the top of the **Menus** screen, click on the **Manage Locations** tab.

When designers are creating WordPress themes, they design them with menu locations in mind. Most themes will allow a menu at the top of the page, usually under the main site logo, but some themes will have multiple locations designed for menus.

In the Twenty Seventeen theme, there are two possible locations where you can put your menu.

The first location is at the top of the page (the second is designed for social media links), so I've chosen my new legal menu to display there.

Save changes when done.

If you now visit your website, your menu will be visible in the location you chose.

HARLUN LIMITED
My Company Website

Homepage   About Us   Contact   Terms   Privacy Policy

Try clicking items in your menu. You should be taken to the corresponding pages on your site.

If you want, you can try adding the menu to other available locations (only the **social links** location in this theme), just to see where it ends up.

When you have finished playing with your menus and locations, make sure your legal menu is only displayed ONCE on your site.

Since different themes offer different options for menu locations, if you decide to change to a different WordPress theme later, you may have to re-arrange your menu(s).

While menu locations allow easy insertion of menus, you can also add menus to other locations using widgets. For example, I often add a menu into the sidebar of a site, and that requires a widget. We'll look at widgets later.

Creating the Categories

OK, so the site is starting to take shape, but we need to start adding the content that we WANT our visitors reading. This is where we start adding posts. Before we do that, we need to set up some categories which will be the filing system for these posts.

Setting up the Categories

I always like to start by creating the first few categories for the posts I know I want to write. You can create categories on the fly, as you need them. However, since I have already planned my site, I know three categories I will be using. Remember this:

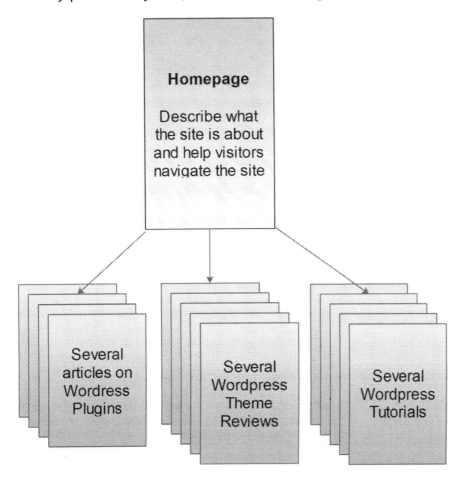

So, I have categories for:

1. Plugins
2. Themes
3. Tutorials

Let's set up those categories now. They won't appear on the site until a post is added to the category, so you don't end up with empty categories.

Click **Categories** under the **Posts** menu in the left sidebar.

On the right of the categories screen, you can see a list of all existing categories. The only one you have now is **Uncategorized**. This is the one that WordPress set up to be used as a default category. If you enter a post and forget to select a category, WordPress would choose this one by default.

I want my "tutorials" category to be the default category. The easiest way to do this is to edit the "Uncategorized" category.

If you move your mouse over "Uncategorized", a menu appears:

Click **Edit**.

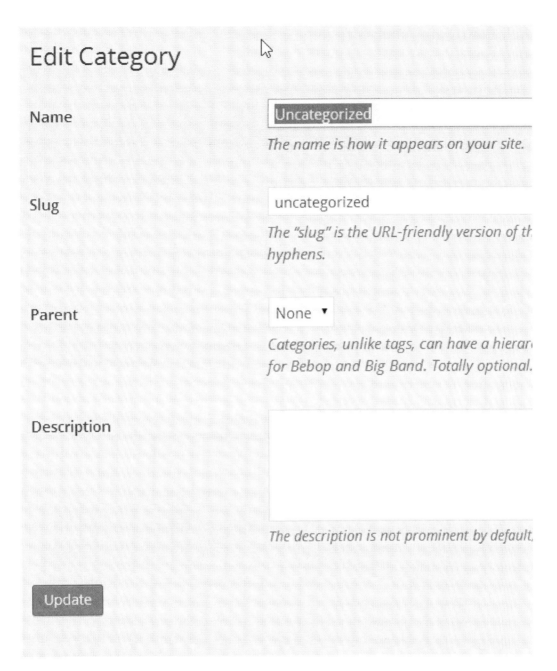

Edit Category

Name

Uncategorized

The name is how it appears on your site.

Slug

uncategorized

The "slug" is the URL-friendly version of th
hyphens.

Parent

None ▼

Categories, unlike tags, can have a hierar
for Bebop and Big Band. Totally optional.

Description

The description is not prominent by default

Update

You can now edit this category.

Enter the name of your chosen default category. In my case, it's "tutorials".

Delete the contents of the **Slug** box, and leave it empty. The slug is the text that will be used in the URL of posts in this category. If the slug is blank when you save your category, WordPress will use the category name to create a slug, with spaces being replaced by dashes.

Leave the **Parent** box as **None**. Choosing a parent allows you to nest categories in much the same way we did with menu items when constructing the legal menu. I don't want nested categories, so no "Parent".

In the description box, enter a few sentences to describe the purpose of the category.

When you have finished, click the **Update** button.

If you go back and look at your categories, your new default category will be listed in place of the old "Uncategorized" category:

Note that third column "Slug". WordPress has given my "tutorials" category the slug "tutorials". That is, the same as the category name. This will now create URLs that look like this:

http://mysite.com/tutorials/using-an-image-for-the-logo

Note that you can enter a slug when creating your categories. This can be useful if you want the slug to be different from the category name.

To enter new categories, just add the information on the left side of the **Categories** page and click the **Add New Category** button when done:

Categories

Add New Category

Name

Plugins

The name is how it appears on your site.

Slug

The "slug" is the URL-friendly version of the name. It is usually all lowercase and contains only letters, numbers, and hyphens.

Parent Category

None ▼

Categories, unlike tags, can have a hierarchy. You might have a Jazz category, and under that have children categories for Bebop and Big Band. Totally optional.

Description

This category looks at a range of plugins.

The description is not prominent by default; however, some themes may show it.

Add New Category

Here is my final list of three categories.

I'll add more as and when I need them.

You'll notice that the default category is the one without a checkbox next to it. Since this category cannot be deleted, the checkbox is missing.

OK, I've got the categories to set up. Let's enter the first post.

Creating Posts

Create a new, bank post. To do this, select **Add New** from the **Posts** menu in the left sidebar.

You now have a blank post, ready for entry.

Before you begin, click on the **Screen Options** button at the top right of the screen.

In the drop-down panel that appears, make sure you have the following checked (you can check them all if you want):

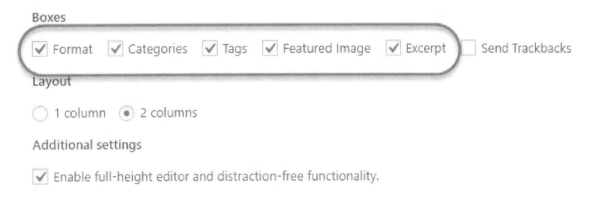

OK, we are now ready to enter a post.

Enter a title

Make sure the title tells the visitor what the post is about, without being overly long. For my first post, I'll call it:

"Recommended Web Hosts and Registrars"

This will be a post about recommended web hosting companies and registrars.

Typing in the post content

You can type your content directly into the WYSIWYG editor, and that is what I do. However, some people prefer to write their content in Microsoft Word first and then copy it across to WordPress. The downside is that you cannot retain formatting from Word, so you'll only be able to paste as plain text. That means reformatting everything once the text is in WordPress.

When you are ready to paste the article into your post, do the following:

1. Select all the text in Word, and copy it.

2. In WordPress, click the **Paste as Text** button. This will strip out extra code from the Word content.

3. Paste into WordPress, and reformat.

Select a category

Once the post is complete, choose a category. I have three to choose from (though I could create another one if needed).

You select the category by checking the appropriate box in the **Categories** section of the **Edit Post** screen:

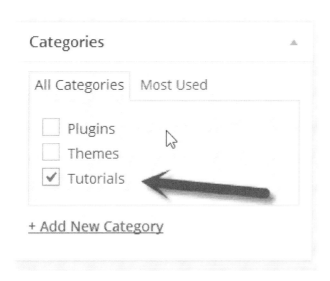

Note that there is an **Add New Category** link underneath the existing categories. This allows you to quickly add other categories when you need them. However, adding a category via this link will not give you the option of adding a category description, so I personally add categories the way I showed you earlier.

Do you need tags?

Since this is my first post, I won't be adding any tags. As I add more posts to the site, I will consider whether they are needed. It is easy enough to go back in and add them to posts, so you don't have to do everything at the time of publishing.

Add an Excerpt

We talked about excerpts earlier in the book. I recommend you add an excerpt for all posts on your site.

Enter a two or three sentence summary of the post. Your visitors will probably read this excerpt as a description of the post on certain pages of your site. Therefore, try to get in their heads and figure out what would make them click through to read the post? Enter that as the excerpt.

Post Formats

Some WordPress themes provide you with a number of "templates" to style each post you create. The Twenty Seventeen theme has several. You'll find them listed in the **Format** section of the **Edit Post** screen:

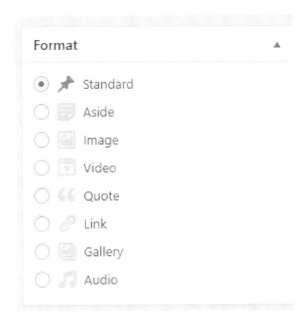

The default format is "Standard" and this is what you should use for most posts on your site. If you select one of the other formats, the layout of that post will change. Each format is designed for a specific purpose, some of which are self-explanatory because of the name of the format. However, since all themes are different, the formats you see above will not be the same in all themes. By all means, try the different formats and visit your post to see the layout of that format.

After exploring these formats, don't forget to go back and change it to "Standard" if that is what you want. Always remember to "Update" your posts after any editing.

OK, everything is entered. Click the **Publish** button to make your post live on your site.

What to do next?

You can now go off and start writing posts on your website. However, as you do, keep an eye on what is happening with your website. For example, the latest posts are displayed on my homepage, with the last published post at the top. I prefer to have a more "static" homepage, without displaying my latest posts like that, so I'll show you how to do that soon.

Have a look at your website.

Is there a sidebar on the homepage?

Is there anything inside the sidebar?

I have several items in my sidebar. These have been added to the sidebar using widgets:

Search... 🔍

RECENT POSTS

Recommended Web Hosts and Registrars

RECENT COMMENTS

ARCHIVES

December 2017

CATEGORIES

Tutorials

META

Site Admin

Log out

In the screenshot above, you can see a widget at the top to add search functionality to the site. Under this are widgets that add **Recent Posts, Recent Comments, Archives, Categories** and finally one called **Meta** which helps login, logout, access RSS feeds, etc.

You have total control over which widgets you want to use in the sidebar. Some themes even allow you to add widgets to other areas of the web page, like the footer.

Let's look at widgets in more detail.

Widgets

From the **Appearance** menu in the left sidebar, select **Widgets**.

Think of widgets as features you can add to your website. We mentioned a few widgets towards the end of the previous section (recent posts, archives, categories etc).

In the Widgets section of the Dashboard, you can see a list of all available widgets, as well as the places you can put them on your website.

The Twenty Seventeen theme gives you three places on your site where you can insert widgets:

1. Blog Sidebar
2. Footer 1
3. Footer 2

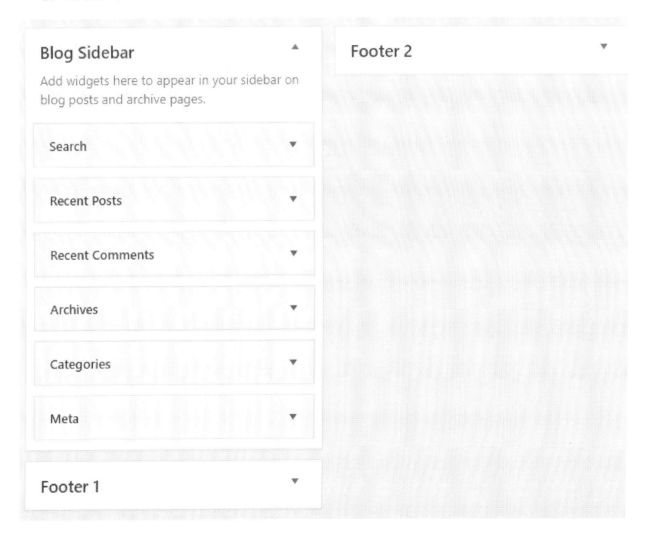

You can see the widgets on the blog sidebar. These are the widgets that added those features to the sidebar in the last section of the book.

Each widget will have some options you can change. These can be accessed by clicking the down arrow on the right of the widget.

For example, here are the options for the Search box:

OK, so the only option is to give it a title. At the moment, there isn't a title, and this is how it looks on my site:

Since the search box has the word "Search" inside, there really isn't a need to give this widget a title. However, feel free to experiment with your own site widgets.

Notice that in the widget options, you also have a delete option if you don't want to use that widget.

The Recent Posts widget has a couple of options:

Again, there is no title specified, yet if we look at the site we see this:

RECENT POSTS

Recommended Web Hosts and Registrars

What? There is a title...

If you leave the title blank for a widget, WordPress will use the default title for that widget, in this case, "Recent Posts". In the case of the Search widget, there was no default title.

If you want to change that title to something else, you can enter a title into your widget options:

Here is what this looks like on my site:

Recommended Web Hosts and Registrars

This widget also lets you choose how many recent posts to display and you can even get the widget to display the dates of each post if you want.

I will leave you to explore the other sidebar widgets that were installed by default.

Open the options and look at how you can configure each widget. Feel free to change settings and see how they affect the display of the widget on the site.

For my site, I don't want recent comments, archives or the Meta widget. Deleting a widget is easy. Open the options for the widget, then click the Delete link.

Note that you can also re-order widgets in the sidebar by dragging and dropping in the Widget screen of the Dashboard. I want to move the Category widget so that it appears right below the search box:

My sidebar looks a lot cleaner:

Search ... 🔍

CATEGORIES

Tutorials

COOL POSTS

Recommended Web Hosts and Registrars

Other widget areas

OK, so we've covered the blog sidebar. However, the Twenty Seventeen theme also allows us to place widgets in the Footer 1 and Footer 2 areas.

Different themes will allow widgets in different areas, so there is little point in going over these widget areas in any detail. The best thing you can do is to put a widget into a widgetized area and see where it appears on your site.

It should come as no surprise if I tell you the two "footer areas" are at the bottom of the web page.

Something to try: Add a Custom Menu widget to a footer area. In the settings of the widget, choose your legal menu. Save, and check out your site.

It is wise to remember that when you add widgets to one of these areas, it will appear on all posts/pages on your site that include that widgetized area. For example, some themes don't include a sidebar on the homepage, but the sidebar is included on all posts. Therefore, a widget placed in the sidebar won't appear on the homepage but would appear on all posts.

There are ways to only include certain widgets in specific categories, posts or pages, but you'll need a WordPress plugin to achieve that. We'll look at one later in this book.

Other available widgets

WordPress installs a basic stock of widgets for you to use and you can experiment with those to see what they do. Some plugins you install will also add new widgets to your dashboard. For example, I often use a plugin called **Formidable Forms**, and when that is installed, it adds a couple of widgets that help insert forms into my web pages:

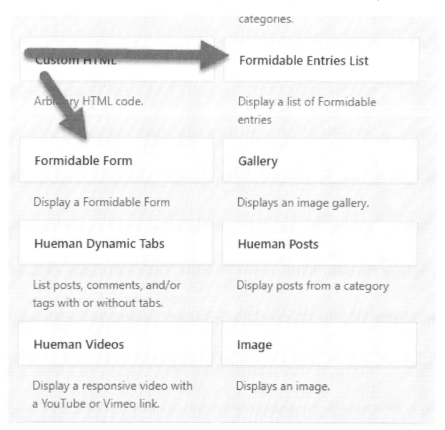

The "Hueman" widgets in that screenshot were added by a WordPress theme, called the Hueman theme.

Have fun experimenting with the widgets, and your theme. We are going to move on and consider a very special page.

The Homepage.

The Homepage - A special case

By default, WordPress will show your recent posts on the homepage. I personally don't like this and prefer total control over what is displayed on my homepage. In fact, I create a page of content to use for my homepage and show that instead of a list of posts. This is easy in WordPress. We simply set up the homepage to show a "static" page.

The first step in achieving this is to create a new WordPress page to use as our Homepage.

Go and click on the **Add New** item in the **Pages** sidebar menu.

Give your page a title that will be displayed at the top of your homepage.

Add the content you want to be displayed on your homepage using the WYSIWYG editor.

After clicking the **Publish** button to make it live, your homepage will still look the same. It still lists the most recent posts...

Don't panic. That's simply because we have not told WordPress to use the new page as a homepage.

To do that, go to the **Reading** settings inside the **Settings** menu in the left sidebar.

Select **A static page** from the **Your homepage displays** section and then choose your newly created page from the **Homepage** drop down box.

Click the **Save Changes** button to finish.

If you now visit the homepage of your site, you'll no longer see your most recent posts in the main area of the homepage. Instead, you will find the WordPress page you just created.

If you see a comment box at the bottom of the homepage, you know how to turn it off. If you don't see a comment form and want one, you know how to turn it on. Personally, I don't include a comment form on my homepage.

You might not like the overall look and feel of your site at the moment. However, later in the book, I'll show you how to change that, any time you like. It only takes seconds and you can choose from an almost unlimited variety of styles.

For now, you should concentrate on adding content to the site. For each category you added, you should add some posts.

While you are working on that, we can consider some other important factors, starting with visitor interaction.

Allowing Comments

I love getting comments from real people wanting to engage me on the site or add their own tips, ideas, or thoughts on a post. However, comments are also a major source of frustration because spammers can flood your inbox with hundreds of automated spam comments. Because of this, a lot of webmasters turn them off. You should not turn them off because real visitors like to comment on your posts. Just as importantly, the search engines love to see a website that actively engages its visitors.

So, what is the problem with spammers and how can we stop them?

Well, if you don't already know, you soon will. Spammers see comments on other people's websites as a way to make their own web pages rank better. You see, when a comment is approved, it links back to the website that was entered into the comment form.

Leave a Reply

Your email address will not be published. Required fields are marked *

Comment

Name *

Email *

Website

Post Comment

So, approved comments are seen as links, and links that point to a site help boost it in Google!

Because of the problems with spammers, we have already set up WordPress so that all comments need to be manually approved. There are also plugins you can install to help cut down on spam comments.

One I like is called WP-SpamShield. Unfortunately, politics being what they are, WordPress removed the plugin from their repository. However, you can still get it on the developer website, but it is no longer free. You can also read their take on why it was removed. Personally, I have been using this plugin for years, and it is the best one out there.

If you prefer to only install plugins from the WordPress repository, then, by all means, search for another anti-spam plugin. I've never found any that work as well as WP-Spamshield.

Let's install it.

You can find the developers website by searching Google for the plugin:

WP-SpamShield Anti-Spam Plugin - Complete WordPress Spam ...
https://www.redsandmarketing.com/plugins/wp-spamshield-anti-spam/
The most advanced anti-spam plugin for WordPress — WP-SpamShield eliminates all WordPress spam: comment spam, contact form spam, trackback / pingback spam, new user registration spam, and more. ... This WordPress plugin includes spam-blocking contact form feature, and protects your ...
WP-SpamShield Removed ... · Configuration Information · Changelog

Go to the website and buy the plugin. You'll download the plugin as a zip file.

We need to upload it to our Dashboard.

On the Add New Plugin screen, click the button to **Upload Plugin**.

You'll need to choose the downloaded plugin zip file, and then click the **Install Now** button.

If you have a plugin in a .zip format, you may install it by uploading it here.

Choose file | wp-spamshield.1.9.21.zip | Install Now

The plugin file will upload. Once complete, click the **Activate Plugin** button.

Once activated, you'll find the WP-SpamShield options inside the Settings menu. Click on it.

You don't need to change anything. Just scroll down until you find the Save Changes button and click on that. If you want to explore the other options (you can download the documentation from the developer site), then please do. Otherwise, rest assured that your site is not being protected from comment spam.

Moderating Comments

We have already seen the comments screen when we looked at the demo comment installed by WordPress, so you should already have a pretty good idea of how this all works.

When someone comes to your site and leaves a comment, it is checked against our blacklist (we set that up earlier). If the comment contains a word or phrase in the blacklist, it is sent to the spam folder. If it passes the checks and also passes the checks by the WP-SpamShield plugin, the comment is added to the "Pending" list. At this point, WordPress sends an email to your admin email address telling you there is a comment to moderate. That email is useful because it contains links to approve, trash, or spam the comment.

```
A new comment on the post "Recommended Web Hosts and Registrars" is waiting for your approval
http://rapidwpsites.com/tutorials/recommended-web-hosts-and-registrars/

Author : My Web Host (IP: 88.18.143.85 , 85.Red-88-18-143.staticIP.rima-tde.net)
E-mail : andy@mywebhost.com
URL    : http://mywebhost.com
Whois  : http://whois.arin.net/rest/ip/88.18.143.85
Comment:
Give me a link back.

Approve it: http://rapidwpsites.com/wp-admin/comment.php?action=approve&c=3
Trash it: http://rapidwpsites.com/wp-admin/comment.php?action=trash&c=3
Spam it: http://rapidwpsites.com/wp-admin/comment.php?action=spam&c=3
Currently 1 comment is waiting for approval. Please visit the moderation panel:
http://rapidwpsites.com/wp-admin/edit-comments.php?comment_status=moderated
```

You can click the relevant link in the email to moderate the comment if you like. I personally like to log into the Dashboard to moderate comments. When you log in to your Dashboard and there are comments waiting, you will see a visual indicator of comments awaiting moderation:

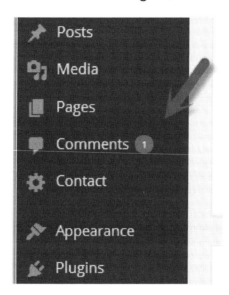

Clicking on the **Comments** menu item takes you to the moderation screen.

Move your mouse over a comment and a menu appears:

From there, you can approve the comment, or send it to spam or trash.

I highly recommend that you are very strict about approving comments. If you do not know the commenter (i.e. they are not a friend or a frequent visitor you know of), then never approve a comment that does not add to the conversation on the post they are commenting on.

For example, on my web hosting post, I would trash all of the following comments:

"Love the site, great work!"

"What theme are you using, it looks great".

"I love this site"

"Fantastic article. I will send my friend over to read it".

"I think you have a problem with browser compatibility".

Incidentally, these are all very common spam comments whose sole purpose is to get a link back to a website. Quite often, spam comments try to flatter you into approving them.

Do you see how none of these are about web hosting? These comments could have been made on ANY post. That is often the sign of a spammer at work.

I tend to only approve comments that add to the "discussion" started by the post. I'd also approve a comment that was obviously written by someone who had read the post and wanted help or advice related to the post. Comments are there for you to interact, help and discuss with your audience. Any comment that does not add to the conversation should be trashed.

When you have comments in the trash, or spam folders, you will eventually need to go in and empty the trash (or empty the spam folder). Just click on the tab (in the screenshot below I have clicked onto the **Trash** tab):

Then click the Empty Trash button.

On the spam screen, there is an "Empty Spam" button.

So, what is the difference between spam and trash?

Well, there isn't a lot of difference. WordPress and many anti-spam plugins will send suspicious comments to the spam folder as a place to hold them until you moderate them. Everything in the spam folder will be suspicious, so have a quick glance down to see if there is anything worth approving. Some anti-spam plugins will check IP and email addresses of comments in the spam folder, and send any further comments from those "spammers" directly to the spam folder.

If there is anything worth approving, you can move your mouse over the comment, and click the "Not Spam" link.

That will send it to the Pending tab.

From there, you can approve the comment if you want.

Social Sharing?

You put a lot of effort into your website, so wouldn't it be nice to give your visitors an easy way for them to share your content with their friends?

Social sharing plugins make this easy.

There are a huge number of different social sharing plugins to choose from. We'll install a popular one here.

Click **Add New** from the Plugins sidebar menu.

Search for **Social Pug**.

Find, install, and activate, this one:

You'll find the plugin adds a **Social Pug** menu directly into the left sidebar.

Click on the Social Pug link.

You have a couple of options in terms of where the sharing buttons appear. You can have a floating sidebar that "floats" on the side of your web page, displaying the buttons. You can also have inline buttons that appear before or after your content. I am going to choose both, to show you what they look like.

When you activate one of the two options, the **Settings** for that option become available:

Click the settings link, and you get more options.

The first thing you need to do is select the networks you want to use:

When you click the **Select Networks** button, you get to choose from the most popular sharing sites:

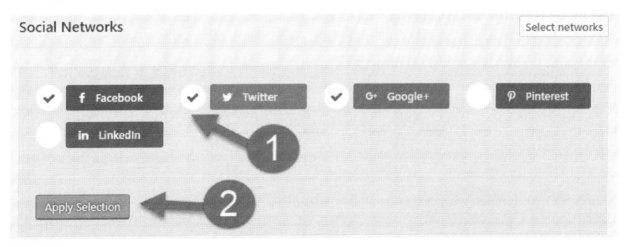

Check the sites you want to include, then click the **Apply Selection** button.

Your chosen networks will appear in a list (that you can re-order by dragging and dropping).

Below this list, you can choose a number of options for the style of button. I will leave you to explore those yourself. However, at the bottom, an important setting is this one:

If you want the social sharing buttons on pages as well (especially if you are using a static page for the homepage), then make sure you check the **Page** type too and save changes.

If you now visit a web page on your site, you should see the social buttons "floating" as you scroll down the page:

If you have selected **Inline** buttons, click on the **Inline Content** link in the menu, and configure those in the same way. Here are some I did earlier 😊

Discounts on ALL of my Udemy courses

Below you'll find a list of all of my courses. If you want to be notified of new courses, or special course promotions, p

WordPress SEO

These buttons are shown before the content of my page. Note that you can show different buttons on inline and floating panels if you want to.

Your visitors can click these buttons to share your post on Facebook, Twitter, Pinterest, Google Plus, etc. This, in turn, can bring more traffic to your site from these social networks.

Website Navigation

Someone landing on your website for the first time will have no idea what content is on your site or how to find it. It is therefore vital that you have good website navigation.

On sites I build, I make sure the following navigation is in place:

1. A homepage that tries to help the visitor find what they want. That can literally mean writing out instructions, using graphics, or just making the sidebar and menu navigation speak for itself.
2. A search box. This is already installed on the site as a widget. The default search box that comes with WordPress is poor. A better option is to add a custom Google search box which offers far more relevant search results from your site. It is beyond the scope of this book to show you how to do this, but Google it, if interested.
3. A Main menu offering contact, about and other "legal" pages. This does not always need to be in the header area of your site. I often put this type of menu in the footer widget area.
4. A recent posts widget in the sidebar of my site. Visitors can quickly see the recent articles I have written, and use those as a starting point for investigating my site.
5. Every post on my site will have a related posts section, which lists other posts that I think a visitor may be interested in.

The only one on that list we have not seen so far is the related posts plugin. Let's install and configure that now.

Select **Add New** from the **Plugins** menu.

In the search box, search for **related posts**.

This is the one you need to find, install and activate:

You will now have a new menu in the Settings:

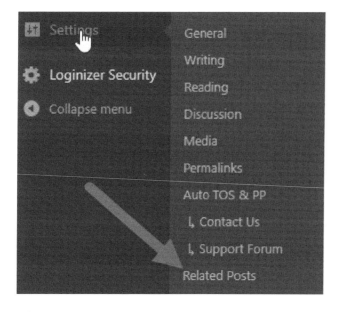

Click on Related Posts to visit the plugin settings.

There are a lot of settings for this plugin, but I'll let you explore most of them. The following are a list of changes I suggest you make to get the plugin up and running on your website:

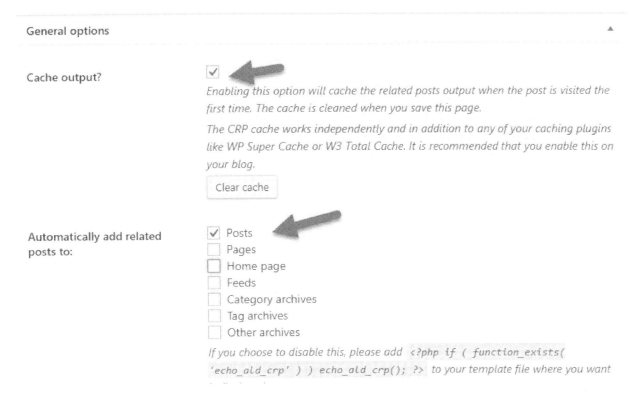

General options ▲

Cache output? ✓

Enabling this option will cache the related posts output when the post is visited the first time. The cache is cleaned when you save this page.

The CRP cache works independently and in addition to any of your caching plugins like WP Super Cache or W3 Total Cache. It is recommended that you enable this on your blog.

Clear cache

Automatically add related posts to:

- ✓ Posts
- ☐ Pages
- ☐ Home page
- ☐ Feeds
- ☐ Category archives
- ☐ Tag archives
- ☐ Other archives

If you choose to disable this, please add `<?php if ( function_exists( 'echo_old_crp' ) ) echo_old_crp(); ?>` *to your template file where you want*

Now scroll down to the first **Save options** button, and click on it to save these settings.

The related posts are now active. Here is an example from one of my sites:

Related Posts:

As you can see, the related posts show up as thumbnails. If you prefer text-based listings, scroll down to the **Styles** section of the settings and select **Text Only**.

Again, save options.

This is what mine looks like now:

Related Posts:

- Chester City & Cathedral
- Crocodile at Oasis Park Fuerteventura
- Barn Owl at Oasis Park – Fuerteventura
- Giraffe at Oasis Park – Fuerteventura
- Zebras at Oasis Park – Fuerteventura
- Bald Eagle at Oasis Park – Fuerteventura

OK, that's it from me. Tweak away as much as you like, and explore the other options. As of now, you have a functioning related posts section at the end of every post.

Note that if there are no related posts for a post, nothing will be displayed.

Keeping WordPress Updated & Secure

WordPress is updated frequently to:

1. Add new features.
2. Fix bugs in the older version.

While some bugs are inconvenient but harmless (e.g. a feature not quite working as it should), others cause security problems for your site. Very occasionally a bug is found that could allow hackers to get into your website, through a "back door". These types of bugs need to be fixed as soon as possible and are usually fixed within hours of being found.

Fortunately, these bugs are rare, BUT, it does mean that you should always keep WordPress updated to the latest version.

When you installed your site, you may have had the option to enable an auto-upgrade script, so upgrades will be largely automatic.

If you don't have automatic updates "switched on", don't worry. Upgrading manually is very easy.

When you log in to the Dashboard, there is an **Updates** item in the **Dashboard** menu.

This will notify when there are updates available, much like the notification we saw earlier with comments to moderate. You can then click through to the **Updates** area, and update the files.

The "Updates" area lists all available updates for WordPress itself, plugins and themes.

When a WordPress upgrade is available, you'll see something like this:

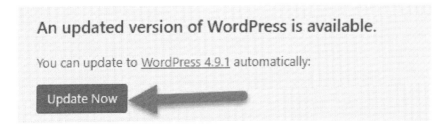

Just click the **Update Now** button and the upgrade will proceed automatically on its own. You may have to click a button or two to "upgrade the database" or some other task, but that's as technical as it gets. Just follow the instructions on the screen and you'll be fine.

If there are plugins to update, you'll see something like this:

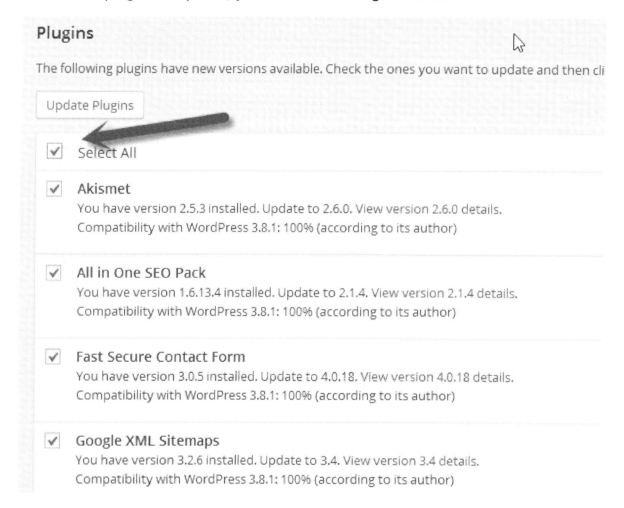

You can check one or more plugins to update, or click the **Select All** checkbox, which selects all plugins for updating. Then, simply click the **Update Plugins** button, and WordPress does the rest for you.

When your theme(s) needs updating, you'll see something like this:

Check the box next to the theme(s) you want to update, and click the **Update Themes** button.

Backing up the Site

Backing up anything on a computer should be a priority. While good web hosts do keep backups for you, if your site gets infected with any kind of malicious code, and you don't find out about it for a while, all of your backups can be infected, and therefore not much use.

I always recommend you have some kind of backup plan, and fortunately, there is a great plugin that can help.

Click the **Add New** item in the **Plugins** menu.

Search for Updraft.

Find, install and activate this plugin:

You'll have a new UpdraftPlus Backups section in the settings menu. Click on it to access the settings of this plugin.

You can take manual backups on the **Current Status** tab of the settings.

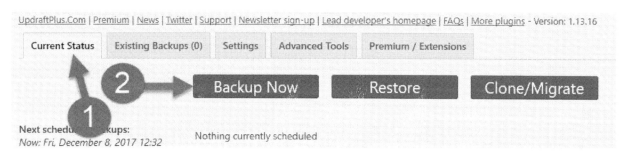

More powerful still is the ability to schedule automatic backups of your site. To do that, click on the **Settings** tab.

Choose a frequency and the number of backups to retain.

Now scroll down and click the **Save Changes** button at the bottom.

You will notice that on this screen, you also have the option of using remote storage for your backups. If you have a Dropbox account, that is a great place to send backups. You can also get them emailed to you. I won't go into details on setting this up, just follow the instructions that are included with the plugin.

Changing the Look & Feel of the site

By now you should have a fully functioning website and know how to add more content to the site. However, you might not like the look of your site. Maybe the colors, the fonts, or the layout, don't look right to you. That is where themes come in.

WordPress was created to be modular in nature so that developers could create add-ons. We've seen some of these in the form of plugins and widgets, but another major way you can customize your site is by changing the WordPress theme.

Think of themes as skins. You can add a skin over the top of your content, which changes the look and feel, but doesn't touch your underlying data (content, installed plugins, etc.).

The quickest way to experience themes is to look at the ones WordPress installed on your server when you installed WordPress.

Go to **Themes** in the **Appearance** menu of your Dashboard.

Here you should find Twenty Seventeen and some possibly a couple of other default WordPress themes.

You can change the theme to one of the other installed themes, quickly and easily.

When you move your mouse over a theme thumbnail, it changes to include two buttons. A **Live Preview** button allows you to see what the theme would look like IF you activated it, and an **Activate** button to change to that theme.

Go ahead and change themes, then visit your homepage to see how different it looks.

Note that when you switch between themes, you may need to move your widgets around after the switch, or even re-add them. This is because all themes are different and have different widget areas, with different names. WordPress does its best when you switch themes but often doesn't get it quite right.

With any theme you want to use, you need to check to see where you can add widgets. Another thing to check is how many menus it can accommodate, and where those menus are located.

Where to get free themes

WordPress makes it easy for you to find and install themes for your site.

Click on **Themes** in the **Appearance** menu.

At the top of the Theme page, click the **Add New** button.

You will be taken to an "Add Themes" screen.

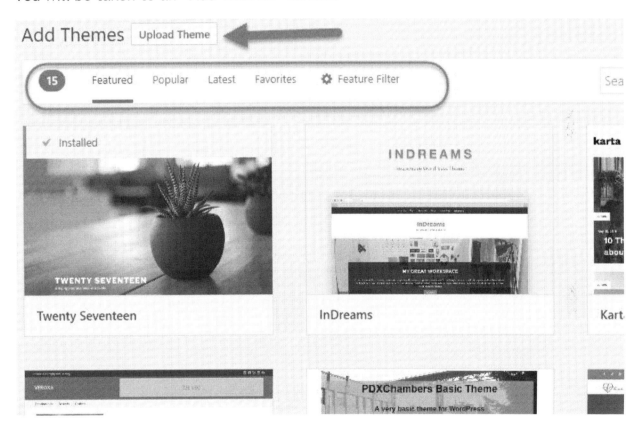

At the very top of this screen is an Upload Theme button. If you've bought or downloaded a theme from a website, it will be zipped up. Just click the Upload Theme button and upload the zipped file. The theme will install and you can then preview or activate it.

Next, on this screen, you'll see a menu across the top, with "Featured" selected. This menu gives you access to "Featured", "Popular" and "Latest" themes in the WordPress repository. Click the menu item that interests you, and browse the themes.

The final option in the menu is the "Feature Filter". This is where you can filter out the free themes according to features you want to have.

For example, if I wanted to search for a three-column theme that allows a custom header, then I'd search for:

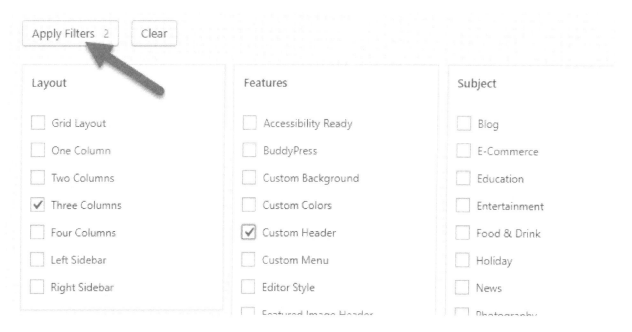

On clicking the **Apply Filters** button, any matches are displayed and appear in the search results:

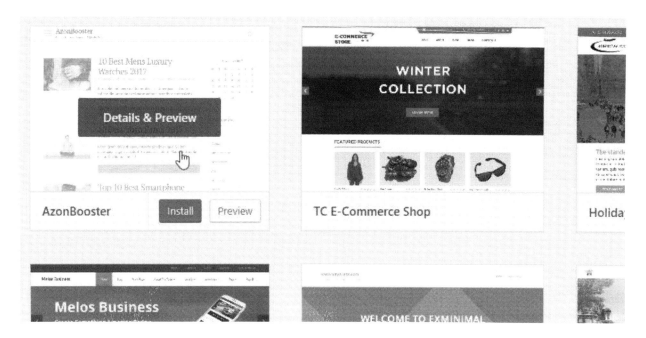

Mouse over each theme in turn to show details for the theme. From this preview, you can:

1. Click **Details & Preview** (or just the Preview button) to get more information about the theme, including a preview.
2. Click the **Install button** to install the theme into your Dashboard.

Note that when you install a new theme, your old one remains in the dashboard. This makes it easy to switch between themes you've installed.

The biggest problem with a lot of free themes is that they have a link back to the creator's website in the footer. This is bad from a search engine point of view, and I do not recommend you use any theme that forces this link on your site.

The WordPress themes we saw earlier do contain links to WordPress, but that is a little different. WordPress is a huge authority site, the creators of the theme and creators of your content management system (CMS). Besides, you can remove that link if you want to.

Customizing a theme

WordPress has a simple point and click interface to help you customize your active theme. However, the customizations that are available to you are dictated by the theme itself. Some themes have very few customizations, while others will offer you pages and pages of custom settings.

There are a couple of ways you can get to the Customize screen. The first is by clicking the **Customize** button on the thumbnail of the active theme in the Themes screen:

The second method is by using the sidebar menu of the Dashboard, where you will find **Customize** in the **Appearance** menu:

Both of these options will open up the "customize" screen:

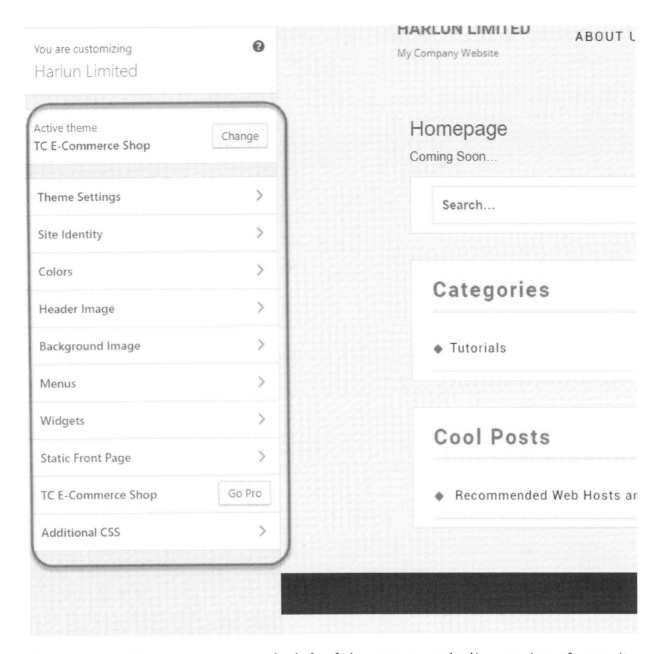

The customization options are on the left of the screen, and a live preview of your site on the right. This allows you to tweak your theme and immediately see the effects of those tweaks in the live preview.

Many of the customizations available here are also accessible via the standard sidebar menus in WordPress (mainly through the **Settings** menu).

Remember that these customization options are specific to the theme you are using. You may see different options for your theme.

The options are grouped into related items. To open these groups, click on the little arrow to the right of the group name. You can explore these options for yourself, but I will mention a couple of items on this customize screen.

Header Image

On this screen, you will be given the dimensions for the header image your theme needs. Make sure your image is sized to those exact dimensions or your header image will look distorted.

The theme above requires a header image of 1600 x 400 pixels. If you are looking to add a completely different shaped logo, you may need to find a theme that can accommodate your image.

Additional CSS

Although CSS is beyond the scope of this book, if you know how to use CSS, you can add custom CSS to style your web pages in this section of the customize options:

```
/*
You can add your own CSS here.

Click the help icon above to learn more.
*/
```

The CSS you add to this box will override the CSS that is built into your theme.

Go through the rest of the options on the customize screen. You won't break anything in this area of WordPress, so have fun and explore.

An Alternative Website Structure

If I was building out the WordPress tutorials site discussed in this book, I would choose a site structure similar to that shown below:

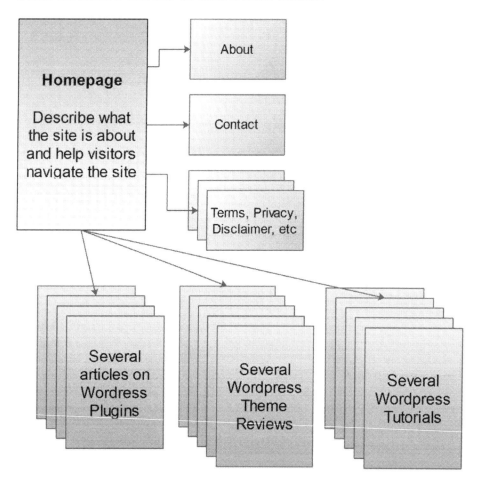

We have a homepage, several "legal" pages, and a few categories, each containing relevant posts.

However, there is another structure that some people prefer, and I want to show you how to set that up. Let's look at a diagram of this structure:

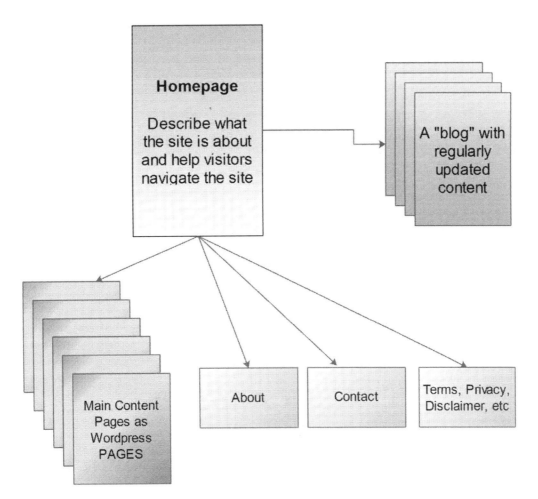

Where this structure is different, is that the main content pages of the site use WordPress pages, not posts. WordPress posts are used as a blog "attached" to the main site.

This type of site is typically a small site, with 5 or 6 main content "static" pages plus legal pages. The blog is then used for regular updates on any topic relevant to the blog.

Let's look at an example.

If you were an author, a small website could help showcase your books and offer a little more information about you and your interests to your readers. A contact form would allow your readers to have direct contact with you, and comments on posts would allow a two-way dialogue (a unique opportunity for many authors, since most never get to meet the people that buy their books).

You might want to have the following pages on your site:

- About
- Contact

- My Books
- Events

These could all be set up as WordPress Pages because they are all fairly independent of one another.

You might then want to have a blog where you can post short stories, interesting anecdotes, interesting background information on stories you are writing, etc. If these were done with posts, your visitors could then leave comments and interact with you and give you feedback on your work.

In this scenario, it makes perfect sense to use WordPress pages for the small number of static pages on your site, and WordPress posts for more regular updates and interacting with your readers.

We already know how to set up pages, so setting up the basic structure of this site is easy. Just create a WordPress page for each of those 4 pages we mentioned above.

For the blog, you might just like to use one category or several. This will depend on what you intend to do with the blog. Whatever you choose, WordPress makes it easy to showcase your blog postings.

The first step is to create a new WordPress Page called "Blog" (or whatever you want to call it). Leave the contents of the page empty and publish it.

Now, under the **Settings** menu, click **Reading**.

In the same way we set the homepage to be a static page, we can set a static page to showcase our "posts", which in this case is the author's "blog" section.

Just select your Blog page from the **Posts page** section of the form, and save changes.

The author could now create the website top navigation menu to include a link to the blog page. Visitors clicking on that would see all of the latest blog posts (from all categories if there is more than one) in chronological order, starting with the most recent.

This is the menu bar from the site of an author I know:

He has used WordPress pages for his About, Books, Interests, Links, Contact & Disclaimer. He then created a WordPress Page to host his blog posts and added all of these pages to the top navigation menu.

Even though one page is dedicated to all blog posts, if you use multiple categories for your posts, you can still use a category widget (if you want to) to help your visitors find specific posts.

NOTE: Anyone can set up a "Blog" page if they want a single location to display all recent posts in chronological order. On a traditional WordPress site where the latest 10 posts are shown on the homepage, this type of blog page is not really needed because your homepage acts as a blog page. However, if you use a static page for your homepage, then a blog page might be useful for your visitors.

Beginner's Mistakes

There are a number of simple mistakes that beginners make when they build a site with WordPress. This chapter lists some of those mistakes.

Post & Page Titles

No two posts should have the same title on your site. No two pages should have the same title either. A post should not use the same title as a page, and vice versa. All post and pages must have unique titles.

If you use the same title on two documents, Google will think you have two articles on the same topic and wonder why. When Google starts getting confused about the content on your site, you are at the beginning of a very slippery slope.

In addition, if you give two posts the same title, the filename automatically generated by WordPress will mean both filenames are nearly the same. WordPress handles duplicate filenames by adding numbers to the end. If you created three pages with the title "contact", WordPress would give them these filenames:

1. Contact
2. Contact-1
3. Contact-2

Tags & Category Names

Never use the same word or phrase for a category name AND a tag. A phrase can be EITHER a category OR a tag, but not both.

Similarly, never use a word or phrase that you have used as a page/post title as either a tag or category.

For example, suppose you had a health site.

If you had a category called diabetes, you could not use the word diabetes as a post/page title, or a tag. You could have a page/post title or tag that included the word diabetes as a longer phrase, like "gestational diabetes", or "pre-diabetes".

Using Tags

Never use more than 4 or 5 tags on a post. Tags should be there to help visitors, so giving visitors long lists of tags will make them useless. Also, indiscriminate use of tags means you'll end up with a lot of tag pages, each listing very few posts. Remember what I said earlier in the book. No tag should be used if it is only being used on one post (or two, and maybe even three depending on the size of your site).

Privacy Settings

There is a setting in WordPress that will basically make your site invisible to the search engines.

Go to **Reading** in the **Settings** menu.

This checkbox is there to stop search engines finding, spidering, and including your site in the search results. Some webmasters use this when they are initially building a site, and then uncheck it when they want to open the site to the public. However, this is not necessary. I'd recommend you leave this unchecked at all times.

If you do find that your site isn't getting indexed and included in Google, do check this setting.

Spam Comments

Over the years, I have seen a number of my students committing this sin. They'll approve a comment on their site, simply because the comment is flattering to them. We've talked about this type of comment before. My advice to you is simple. No matter how few comments you may have, NEVER approve a comment that does not add to the conversation of the post it will appear on.

NEVER!

Plugins for all occasions

We have already installed and used some great WordPress plugins. However, there are thousands more out there. In this chapter, I'll list the plugins that I have found to be the most useful on my own sites. Some of these plugins are used on all of my WordPress sites, while others are only used for more specific projects.

To keep this book shorter, I will list the most important plugins I use regularly, with a description of what they do.

Yoast SEO

Yoast SEO is a free plugin that can help you set up your site with the search engines in mind. SEO stands for Search Engine Optimization, and although we have to be careful implementing SEO strategies on our sites, this plugin is well worth installing. It is an extremely feature-rich plugin that gives you a fine level of control over all posts, pages, tag pages, category pages, etc. I use this on every site I build.

Find it in the plugin repository.

Pretty Link Lite

Pretty Link Lite is a free plugin that allows you to create "prettier" links from longer, "uglier" links. It also allows you to track links.

Why might you want to do this?

We'll mention affiliate programs in the next chapter, and these have notoriously ugly long links. Pretty Link Lite is a great way to make those links more manageable.

Find it in the plugin repository.

Formidable Pro

Formidable Pro is a commercial plugin that allows you to create just about any type of web form for your site. While it is overkill for a simple contact form, I use this plugin to allow visitors to submit information to me, like images, guest posts, etc. Formidable Pro gives me total flexibility.

http://ezseonews.com/formidablepro

CI Backlinks

CI Backlinks is a commercial plugin that I helped develop, which automates internal site linking in the body of your articles. Internal site links help your visitors find their way around your site (check out this type of linking on Wikipedia) but also help the search engines spider your site, and decide what the web pages on your site are about.

http://ezseonews.com/cibacklinks

Dynamic Widgets

Dynamic widgets is a free plugin that allows you to choose specific pages, posts, categories etc. to display widgets on. I use this on most of my sites so that I can create custom sidebars for different categories on the site. If someone is reading a post on my site about web hosting, I can make sure that they see web hosting related advertising in the sidebar.

I also usually create a unique sidebar for my homepage.

I believe that Google prefers websites that don't have the exact same sidebars & footers on all web pages. This plugin helps you achieve that since you can control which widgets appear on which pages, and in which widgetized areas of the page.

Find it in the plugin repository.

W3 Total Cache

W3 Total Cache is a free plugin to speed up your site. It is a little complicated to set up but well worth the effort.

Find it in the plugin repository.

Wishlist Member

Wishlist Member is a commercial plugin that allows you to set up a membership site (paid or free) on your website. I use it for the training programs and courses that I create.

https://ezseonews.com/wlm

SimplePress

Simplepress is a free plugin that allows you to set up a forum on your site. If you want to grow a community on your website, this plugin can create a forum on your site, with a few mouse clicks.

Making Money with your website

There are a lot of different ways you can make money with your website. I won't go into too much detail in this book, but I will briefly discuss the options.

All of the following forms of site monetization are free to join and do not cost anything to run on your website.

Affiliate programs

An affiliate program (sometimes called a partner program) is a good way to make some money from your site. A lot of great companies run them, and you can apply to join relevant programs.

Amazon has a great affiliate program. When you join, you can link to any product on the Amazon website from your own website, using a link that Amazon gives you. This link is long and ugly, which is where Pretty Link Lite comes in. If someone goes through your link and buys something, you get a commission.

The amount of commission you get with affiliate programs varies enormously. For example, Amazon pays around 4% - 8% of the order value, but they convert customers very well.

Other sites like Clickbank specialize in digital products (eBooks & software). The average commission is probably around 50%, but you can earn 75% commission on some products, sometimes even more than that.

Shareasale and Commission Junction are two affiliate networks I use. An affiliate network is a company that works with other companies that want to run an affiliate program. You can sign up at Shareasale and/or Commission Junction (often just referred to as CJ), then apply to join affiliate programs on their books. Some affiliate programs will accept you immediately; others require a manual review of your site and application. However, it is typically very easy to join affiliate programs through both of these networks. If you make a commission on a network, the network collects the commissions for you and then pays you every month.

Google Adsense

When you visit Google and search for something, the top few results are typically adverts related to what you searched for. Companies are paying for these adverts.

If you click on one of these adverts in Google, the company that paid for the advert pays Google some money. The amount they have to pay is based on the "cost per click" (or CPC) value of that advert. Adverts in more competitive niches cost more, so the CPC is higher.

Google Adsense is a program that allows you to put similar "Adsense" adverts on your website. When someone clicks on one of these Adsense adverts on your site, Google gets paid the CPC by the company that owns the advert. Google then share this money with you.

Where to go for more help

This book covered the basics of getting a website up and running. I know you will love WordPress, and many of you will want to do more with it than I was able to cover in this book. That is why I added this section to my website:

http://ezseonews.com/wp

It serves as a way for you to contact me, and ask for specific tutorials. If you want to see how to do something, contact me directly on the site.

More information from Dr. Andy Williams

If you would like more information, tips, tutorials or advice, consider signing up for my free newsletter over at ezSEONews.com offering tips, tutorials, and advice to online marketers and webmasters. My newsletter, plus SEO articles, etc. will be delivered to your inbox. I cannot always promise a weekly schedule, but I do try ;)

My other Webmaster books

All my books are available as Kindle books and paperbacks. You can view them all here:

http://amazon.com/author/drandrewwilliams

I'll leave you to explore those if you are interested. You'll find books on various aspects of being a webmaster such as creating high-quality content, SEO, CSS etc.

My Video Courses

You can view a complete list of my video courses here:

http://ezseonews.com/udemy

There are courses on the same kinds of topics that my books cover, so SEO, Content Creation, WordPress, Website Analytics, etc.

Did you enjoy this book?

If you liked this book (or even if you didn't), PLEASE add a review on the Amazon website. It provides me with valuable feedback and helps prospective students decide whether it is the right book for them.

All the best

Andy Williams

Made in the USA
San Bernardino, CA
17 February 2018